THE YOUTH TRAINING SCHEME IN THE UNITED KINGDOM

KU-580-455

The Youth Training Scheme in the United Kingdom

PAUL G. CHAPMAN
and
MICHAEL J. TOOZE
Department of Economics,
The University, Dundee

Avebury

Aldershot · Brookfield USA · Hong Kong · Singapore · Sydney

© P.G. Chapman and M.J. Tooze,1987

All rights reserved. No part of this publication may be reproduced ,stored in a retrieval system, or transmitted in any form or by any means, electrical, mechanical, photocopying, recording, or otherwise without prior permission of the Gower Publishing Company Limited.

Published by

Avebury

Gower Publishing Company Limited,
Gower House, Croft Road, Aldershot, Hants GU11 3HR,
England

Gower Publishing Company,
Old Post Road, Brookfield, Vermont 05036
United States of America.

British Library Cataloguing in Publication Data

Chapman, Paul G.
The Youth Training Scheme in the United Kingdom.
1. Youth Training Scheme
I. Title II. Tooze, M.J.
331.3'412042 HD6276.G7

ISBN 0-566-05360-8

Printed in Great Britain by
Richard Clay & Company Limited, Bungay, Suffolk

Contents

Acknowledgements

The initial employers' survey was carried out for the Scottish Council, Development and Industry and the re-interview survey was funded by the Economic and Social Research Council.

We wish to thank the Department of Employment, Manpower Services Commission and the Editor of Youth Training News for the willing assistance given to us in the preparation of this volume.

It would be wholly appropriate to acknowledge also our debt to the many employers and representatives of other organisations who were prepared to give up time to be interviewed, in depth , about the Youth Training Scheme.

There are many others who contributed to this volume. In particular we would like to mention Betty Barty and Dorothy Hargreaves for typing the manuscript. We are grateful to them for their help and patience.

August,1986

Paul G Chapman
Michael J Tooze

List of tables and chart

1 Introduction

The Youth Training Scheme (YTS) was launched in April 1983. This study examines the background to its development and also the economic effectiveness of the Scheme.

Three aims of the Scheme were originally identified by the Manpower Services Commission (MSC). These were to provide a training option for school leavers, to increase the productivity of firms by improving the labour skills of the workforce and to increase the flexibility of the labour force for future economic development. These objectives and the structure of the YTS are discussed in detail in Chapter Six.

In a wider context it might be argued that the development of the YTS is in response to recent declines in training and increases in unemployment. First, it represents a response to the decline in training in the United Kingdom which has occurred throughout the seventies and particularly in the early eighties. This decline is described in more detail in Chapter Three. Second, it is also clear that the United Kingdom training initiative is part of a general European response to the decline in training. The European Commission has been urging Member States to review and reform vocational training programmes and through the European Social Fund has provided funds for this purpose

(HMSO, 1984, p.xiii). Third, the YTS provides a mechanism for delaying entry into the labour market by providing all school leavers with a "job experience" alternative to either unemployment or an unwilling extension of full-time education. The various employment and training schemes of the post-war period are reviewed in Chapters Four and Five, and the YTS can, in part, be seen as an extension of previous efforts to respond to the particular difficulties of the youth labour market. In this sense it is still an aid to employment as well as a training initiative, particularly when viewed in conjunction with the recently introduced New Workers Scheme.

The general thrust of the following discussion subdivides into three main sections. The principal economic considerations underlying the analysis of training are reviewed in Chapter Two. Chapters Three, Four , Five and Six are devoted to a historical and institutional discussion of employment and training measures and trends in the United Kingdom in recent years. Chapter Seven contains an appraisal of the YTS and draws on the findings of two employers' surveys where information is not available from other published sources. The scope and structure of these surveys are described below.

THE SURVEY EVIDENCE

The surveys were carried out in 1984 and 1985 among employers who were providing on-the-job training for Mode A schemes in the Dundee and Renfrew local labour markets. The original survey was undertaken in May-June 1984 as part of a larger project for the Scottish Council, Development and Industry (Chapman and Tooze, 1985). A re-interview survey was financed by the Economic and Social Research Council and carried out in August-October 1985, by which time details of the two-year YTS had been announced (Chapman and Tooze, 1986). Many of the findings of these surveys have wider geographical relevance as a quarter of the respondents were also providing on-the-job training in England and Wales.

In the absence of a sampling frame at the beginning of the 1984 enquiry, the local MSC offices provided for each district a sample of 60 locations with 297 YTS trainees in total. The establishments represented about 10 per cent of employment in both areas. In selecting these addresses MSC were asked to take account of the industrial structure of the districts, the sizes of establishments and the number of trainees within each establishment.

Biases in the sample surveys

However, inspection of the distribution of observations by industry suggested biases towards the Distributive Trades (Industrial Order XXIII), Miscellaneous (XXVI), and Public Administration (XXVII) and against Professional Services (XXV) in both districts. There was a bias towards Electrical Engineering (IX), Clothing and Footwear (XV) and Bricks, Pottery, Glass and Cement (XVI) in Renfrew and towards Chemicals and Allied Industries (V), Vehicles (XI), Metal Goods (XII), Textiles (XIII), Other Manufacturing Industries (XIX), Construction (XX), and Gas, Electricity and Water (XXI) in Dundee. In 1984 the response rate was 83.0 per cent in Renfrew and 80.0 per cent in Dundee, and in 1985 it was 91.7 per cent in both areas. For comparative purposes the eight employers who did not take part in the re-interview were omitted from the 1984 figures, but this did not affect the basic structure of the sample to any great extent.

Structural features of the sample surveys

There were several similarities in the coverage of the returns from each area in the 1984 survey. First, there was a relatively large number of small establishments with no more than one or two trainees each and a relatively small number of larger establishments with more trainees. Just under 60 per cent of the returns covering just over 25 per cent of the trainees were from establishments employing fewer than 26 people, while about 25 per cent of the returns covering just over 50 per cent of the trainees were from establishments employing more than 100 people (Table 1.1). Second, almost 90 per cent of trainees in each area were employed in only four Occupational Training Families (OTF's). These were Clerical and Administration (OTF1), Installation, Maintenance and Repair (OTF4), Manufacturing and Assembly (OTF6) and Personal Services and Sales (OTF9) (Table 1.2). Third, almost 40 per cent of trainees in each area were employed in establishments that were the sole place of trading, but establishments that were part of an international group were poorly represented (Table 1.3).

Comparisons with the 1985 sample show several differences between the two sets of data. First, the overall number of trainees in the sample was 22.1 per cent lower in 1985 compared with 1984. Second, the 1985 returns showed a substantial shift to Clerical and Administration (from 27.2 per cent in 1984 to 45.9 per cent overall). There was a small reduction in the proportion of trainees in Personal

Services and Sales (from 27.2 per cent to 24.8 per cent) but the main reductions occurred in Installation, Maintenance and Repair (from 20.6 per cent to 10.4 per cent) and in Manufacturing and Assembly (from 13.2 per cent to 5.4 per cent). Third, in 1985 there was a lower proportion of trainees in the smaller-size plants and a higher proportion in the larger-size establishments. Between 1984 and 1985 the overall proportion of trainees in plants with fewer than 26 employees fell from 25.9 per cent to 17.1 per cent, while the percentage of trainees in establishments with more than 250 employees rose from 32.3 per cent to 46.2 per cent. Fourth, between 1984 and 1985 the number of apprentices eligible for the YTS decreased from 23 to 12, and the numbers participating in the YTS fell from 17 to 1.

Underlying these figures is the fact that 54.5 per cent (48) of respondents decreased their numbers of YTS trainees between 1984 and 1985, and 37.5 per cent (33) of the respondents who had trainees in 1984 had none in 1985. 23.9 per cent (20) of respondents reported no change in their number of trainees between 1984 and 1985 and only 21.6 per cent (19) experienced an increase. Of the 48 respondents who experienced reductions in the numbers of trainees in 1984-85, 38 indicated their reasons. The collective responses are summarised in Table 1.4 and point to four main reasons of roughly equal importance and two of lesser significance. Some respondents (8) said that they were not particularly interested in the YTS. In its less extreme version this explanation took the form of doubts about the Scheme and a need for reappraisal of their companies' involvement. The more extreme forms of this position tended to originate from unfortunate experiences with the YTS in the past, such as dissatisfaction with the managing agent or excess absenteeism by the trainees. Several respondents indicated that the low calibre of previous trainees meant that it was not worth all the time and effort involved, and that it was quicker to do the job oneself rather than to try and take time to explain the work in detail. A second reason affecting nine respondents was that neither their premises nor the current volume of business was large enough to provide adequate accommodation for, or supervision of, the trainees. Third, a group of eight employers said that the reduction in the numbers of trainees in 1984-85 was only temporary as they were in the process of change-over between intakes. This is distinguishable from the fourth group (eight respondents) in which participation in the YTS seemed to have passed into a more permanent abeyance in that no trainees had been sent by the MSC or managing agents to fill the places that were available. It might well be that some of these respondents were now regarded as unsuitable by the placement agencies, but there is some evidence to show that this was certainly not so in all cases. Regardless of the suitability of the vacancies this breakdown in communication has given rise to uncertainty among the respondents, and it is arguable that this is harmful to the long term development and acceptance of the YTS. Trade Union opposition and recent redundancies in the adult labour force were less important reasons for reduced participation in the Scheme in 1985.

By way of qualification, it should be added that the overall pattern conceals generally small differences between the YTS structures of the two local labour markets. It is to be expected that the impact of local and exogenous factors on the YTS will increase as the level of geographical disaggregation increases, and that local labour market experiences will be distributed around their corresponding national norms.

2 The economics of training

Historically the economics of training has been relatively neglected by economists, industrialists and governments alike, particularly in the United Kingdom. There has been a tendency to assume that training is worthwhile and attempts to assess in detail its associated costs and benefits have been limited.

The following discussion centres on the economic analysis of training. In this sense the costs and benefits related to training are strictly limited to its output and employment effects, which at least in principle can be measured. No account is taken of the contribution that training might make towards alleviating other social problems. So, for example, the benefits arising from training purely as a break from what has been called "the monotony of unemployment" are excluded from this analysis.

HUMAN CAPITAL THEORY

The economic analysis of training stems from the development of Becker's Theory of Human Capital (Becker, 1964,1975a and 1975b). Blaug has commented that "Becker's analysis is virtually the first serious discussion of on-the-job training in 200 years of Economics, and it has left its mark on the debate about labour training now going on in all advanced countries" (Blaug, Becker's approach considers training as a process of investment leading to the accumulation of human capital. Investment in training by employers and workers will be undertaken to the point at which the present value of expected future returns exceeds costs by an amount sufficient to yield an acceptable rate of return. Investment may take the form of choosing jobs with a high training content,taking time off work for off-the-job training , or learning-by-doing during normal working time (Killingsworth,1983).

General and specific skills

Central to Becker's theory is the distinction between general and specific training. General training raises the worker's marginal productivity in firms other than the one where training takes place, whereas specific training raises the worker's marginal productivity only in the firm where training has been given. Under competitive conditions the worker fully trained in general skills must be paid the value of his marginal product in the firm that trained him. Any attempt by the firm to recoup some of its outlays on training by paying him less would encourage the worker to move to another company where his wage would be equal to the value of his marginal product. Thus the onus is entirely on the trainees, and assuming they are fully informed of present opportunities and future prospects and have full access to capital markets to finance the cost of training, they will invest in training themselves since they will receive a return on it after the training period. This reasoning underlay much of the criticism of the Industrial Training Boards. This is examined in more detail in Chapter Four.

On the other hand the costs of specific training may be shared between the employer and trainee. During the training period the wage paid to the trainee must equal the wage in his best alternative employment, because no rational employee would pay for training that did not benefit him. It therefore follows that wages will exceed the worker's marginal product in the training period, and will be less than the marginal product in subsequent periods so as to enable the firm to recoup its costs. However, if the worker were to quit at the end of the training period the firm's investment would be wasted. Similarly, if the trainee had borne all the costs and received all the returns, he would suffer a capital loss were he to be fired on completion of training. The optimal strategy for the employer is to share some of the costs and benefits of specific training with his employees. This is a situation of bilateral monopoly; the firm is in a monopsonistic position for the purchase of that particular skill and in the short term the employee may be able to exploit his monopolistic position.

However, in practice the concepts of general and specific training are analytical terms representing two poles of a continuum (Thurow,1970). Subject to the proviso that expected returns cover costs by an acceptable margin the extent to which firms move along this continuum depends largely on the degree of market imperfection ,the prevailing economic climate and the nature of any complementarities between human and physical capital. For example, employers will tend to invest more in the general training of workers if there are significant monetary and psychic costs involved in leaving one job and taking another, or where the labour market within the firm is segmented from the external labour market by constraints on hiring or promotion. Employers will tend to invest less in general training in times of recession and where there is an expectation that high levels of unemployment will continue into the foreseeable future. A prolonged recession is likely to affect adversely firms' cash flow positions, and to lower the level of expected future returns from any investment in training. Complementarities between human and physical capital imply that the firm may be able to profit from both general and specific training. The point is that increasing the skills of the labour force raises the returns to both physical capital and labour, because human capital investment increases the stock of labour with which physical capital works. In other words if training raises the marginal productivity of physical capital, companies can earn additional profits from training regardless of whether it is general or specific.

The means of human capital accumulation

Within the human capital framework skill acquisition methods can also be categorised according to the degree of formality involved. They range from formal training through informal training to learning from experience, and can be combined in ways to meet the requirements of individual companies. For example, complex skills requiring detailed instruction and supervised practice because of the high cost of errors and spoilage may demand relatively formal training methods, while simple routine skills requiring little but plenty of practice may be acquired more efficiently by relatively informal means. The notion of learning-by-doing is of particular significance to the present argument. Oatey (1970) has suggested that it is responsible for much skill acquisition in industry, but more recently the discussions on vocational training have extended the concept to encompass the more general aspects of "work experience".

The categorisation of human capital theories on the basis of the degree of informality is important for the assessment of the likely reasons for deficiencies in the overall level of training in the economy. Where learning-by-doing constitutes a small part of the training process training will tend to be associated with relatively low wages because the amount of working time, as opposed to training time, is reduced. On the other hand the greater the role played by learning-by-doing the weaker will be the case for an inverse relationship between wages and training content because working time and training time are the same, and so time spent training is also time spent making the firm's regular output. It follows that the learning-by-doing component of human capital investment will be reduced in times of high unemployment.

The rate of discount

Before the costs and benefits of human capital creation can be evaluated they must be discounted to arrive at an appropriate valuation. With perfect capital markets the market rate of interest (if there is a unique rate) is appropriate. In the absence of any capital constraints the individual will choose to accumulate human capital as long as the net present value is greater than zero at the market rate of interest.

Imperfect capital markets make the market solution much less attractive than it would be in a fully competitive economy because they will result in a higher rate of discount, and capital markets for human capital investment are less likely to reach the competitive level than markets for other goods and services for a number of reasons (Thurow, 1970). Although unlimited amounts of finance cannot be obtained for investment in either human or physical capital, the former is much less liquid than the latter because it can neither be held as collateral nor be sold. Of relevance is the fact that the possession of human capital may also provide the individual with complementary consumption goods in the form of more personal enjoyment and satisfaction, and these are not transferable. Again a lack of knowledge about individual human capital production functions means that banks are less certain of the amount of human capital that their resources will create, and although making large numbers of loans does reduce the problem to some extent it does not eliminate it. The problem is accentuated by the fact that, unlike physical capital investments, banks cannot exert any control over how their loans are used, and individuals cannot be forced to purchase complementary assets or to avoid assets which might reduce the return on their human capital. Also it is desirable to make investments in human capital at an early age to maximise the potential returns, but young people do not possess collateral assets and are relatively risky investments. All these factors tend to increase the risks to lending institutions and reduce their willingness to lend.

These problems are particularly acute for persons with low incomes. If the marginal utility of income rises as income falls, lower income groups will have a higher rate of time preference than the higher income groups because current income is essential for survival and can only be used for investment if future returns are very high. Since the lower income groups cannot afford to devote much of their current income to producing future income they will have a high discount rate and invest less in their human capital than the higher income groups. The alternative is to borrow, but borrowing possibilities may be severely restricted without the security of high current income. Thus those with low incomes tend to invest less in human capital and the cycle is self-perpetuating.

The social rate of discount may differ from the private rate of interest, and too little investment will be undertaken by the private sector if the social rate is lower than the private rate. Society's time horizon may be longer than that of the individual or company and the social rate of time preference will probably be below the private rate of time preference for most groups.

EMPLOYMENT PROSPECTS

The role of vocational training can be related to wider aspects of the overall labour market by distinguishing between the stock of unemployment and the flows of unemployed labour into and out of that stock. In general there are two schools of thought concerning the main determinants of the rate of leaving the unemployment register. First, there are those who believe that personal characteristics are critical and second, there are those who maintain that unemployment duration itself determines re-employability. The personal characteristics school implies a constant probability of leaving the unemployment register for a given worker, and also that this probability is determined by personal characteristics such as conscientiousness and reliability prior to entry on to the register. The duration hypothesis implies that the probability of leaving the register is variable and falls as unemployment duration increases. Thus, it is suggested that people who have experienced longer spells of unemployment are less energetic in their job search and less suitable as recruits to employers because of the depreciation of their skills, particularly those that have been acquired through learning-by-doing. Complicating but not necessarily contradicting these approaches is the impact of labour market conditions.

A more complete account of the macroeconomic aspects of training policies are given in Hughes (1972) who argues that manpower policies may be related to demand management in two ways. First, in so far as the overall level of demand determines the employment prospects of trainees it also determines the social rate of return of training. Second, training policies may have a bearing on some of the "trade-offs" associated with macro-economic policy. For example, training that reduces structural unemployment will shift the Phillips Curve to the left and thereby lower the natural rate of unemployment. Arguably there is a case for any policy that improves these trade-offs, including training policies.

The employment queue

In practice personal characteristics, unemployment duration and labour market conditions interact in determining re-employability. Employers rank potential employees in the form of a queue according to the ease and cost with which they can be integrated into the technical and social organisation of the firm, and the level of economic activity is the major factor in the determination of the length of this queue.

One of the objectives of vocational training is to improve the employability of young people at the start of their working lives with a combination of off-the-job training and work experience. For some young people there will be a tendency for work experience and training to provide an extra dimension to an array of personal characteristics that would already be acceptable to potential employers. For others there will be an additional tendency for vocational training to enrich the personal characteristics themselves and so project them within the range of acceptability to employers.

The training investment

The main economic argument for undertaking training in times of high unemployment is that the lost production or resource cost is low because there is no cost to society in terms of foregone production. On the other hand it is arguable that the return on the investment in vocational training is also likely to be reduced for an economy with insufficient job opportunities for young people completing vocational training courses. Furthermore, the problem of skills depreciation is likely to be compounded in an open economy where a strong domestic market is necessary to exploit economies of scale and lower unit costs in order to complement the gains in comparative advantage provided by an increase in the quality of the labour force. If there exists a general lack of effective demand in the domestic economy, one or more of several possibilities can be envisaged. For example, it might well be that the major impact of vocational training occurs through a partial re-ordering of the queue of trainees with some trainees benefiting at the expense of others. The job prospects for all trainees, however, might be enhanced either if, as a group, they get jobs at the expense of others who are already unemployed or if they opt for training in occupational groupings with a high potential for current employment growth. Although these possibilities might raise the job prospects for particular individuals, none is necessarily satisfactory for the economy as a whole. They either offer little prospect for net job creation or create the danger of a long term bias in the overall skill mix of the economy. It is therefore arguable that the social rate of return on vocational training will be lowered unless there are a sufficient number of appropriate job opportunities.

The finance of training

A second implication of the relatively high current rates of unemployment is the extent to which young people might be able to finance their own training. Those trainees who have not had an opportunity to accumulate savings in the past, or come from social and domestic backgrounds where unemployment is endemic are unlikely to possess the resources necessary for financing training themselves, and these may be the very people whose job prospects are likeliest to be improved by training. It has been seen above that in these circumstances the problems of self-finance will be accentuated by the existence of imperfect capital markets. In general the optimal rate of investment in training will not be achieved because the private rate of return will be below the social rate of return despite the latter being reduced by the lack of demand in the economy.

The dichotomy of the labour market

Many of these relationships in the youth labour market are reflected in the now widely accepted view of a dichotomy in the labour market between "primary" and "secondary" sectors. While the primary market offers jobs with high wages, good working conditions, job security and the possibility of advancement, the secondary market contains the less attractive jobs. The most important characteristic distinguishing jobs between the two sectors is the behavioural requirements which they impose on the workforce, particularly that of employment stability (Doeringer and Piore, 1971). It is therefore workers from the secondary labour market who are most likely to experience the longer durations of unemployment and therefore the greater depreciation of any skills they might have. It also follows that this group is least able to finance training itself. Vocational training may be viewed as a first step in a strategy towards the erosion of this dichotomy.

DISPLACEMENT

A recurring problem in labour market analysis is that as "new employment" occurs as a result of specific policy initiatives the net addition to total employment may only be a proportion of this addition. Chapman and Tooze (1982) explore this problem in the context of redundant employees re-entering employment and displacing other workers in the labour force. It is also sometimes referred to as labour substitution which follows from the notion of one new employee being substituted for another actual or potential employee. More formally, if trainees fill vacancies that would otherwise have been filled by those already unemployed or those changing jobs , displacement occurs. But if the trainees have skills which are available from no other source the vacancies they fill represent non-displacement. Thus in the case of training, the main interest is the extent to which private and public training leads to employment which otherwise would not have come about, and its economic impact in terms of job creation can be assessed in the light of displacement effects.

The expected benefits include the additional temporary employment in the form of the total number of occupied training places minus the number of employees displaced by the trainees, the potential extra long term employment associated with trainees either remaining with their initial employer or gaining a job elsewhere on completion of training and the possible reduction in skill shortages in both the short and long term.

In terms of measuring these displacement effects it is particularly important to focus on the short term impact on employment. It is difficult to identify displacement in the long term because of the presence of other labour market influences. However, even in the short term the measurement problems are forbidding particularly in the identification of skill shortages. Two particular problems arise from the heterogeneous quality of the labour force and the existence of disequilibrium in the labour market. Arguably in a skill market where wages are below equilibrium and skill shortages are observed, the search for measures to reduce these shortages should be limited to wage structure policies where the disequilibrium relationships are self-correcting. Some displacement results for the YTS are included in Chapter Seven.

WAGES AND EMPLOYMENT

The link between wages and employment is an important aspect of any study of youth training. Some of the issues are explored in more detail in Chapter Seven but the general arguments are presented here as a summary of the main features of the debate.

Major areas of contention are the extent to which it is appropriate to refer to a demand curve for labour and whether any such relationship has a relatively high elasticity of demand. There is a wide spectrum of views concerning the strength of the relationship between the price of labour and the level of employment, and while some authorities believe that wages are an important determinant of the demand for labour, others maintain that the relationship is either weak or non-existent. There are two aspects of the view that the demand for labour is relatively elastic. First, in international comparisons it is expected that countries with high youth-adult wage ratios will tend to possess high youth unemployment rates and low levels of youth training. Second, for time-series data it is hypothesised that variations in relative youth unemployment are positively related to variations in the youth-adult wage ratio. Clearly the resolution of these questions is an empirical matter.

In the development of youth employment policies, much attention has been given to the use of wage subsidies as a way of encouraging employers to hire more labour, particularly younger workers. The development of government-financed training schemes like the YTS which provide training for new entrants to the labour market represents a different strategy of intervention, although the use of wage subsidies to lower the relative wages of the youth labour force is still evident in the form of the New Workers Scheme and perhaps represents a more attractive option for those who emphasise an elastic wage-employment relationship. The problems of choosing appropriate wage subsidies are explored further in Chapter Four.

The main difficulty in interpreting wages in the youth labour market is that they are intrinsically bound up with the status of trainees. It is often the case that where youth wages are low, trainees are seen as engaged primarily in learning activities and receiving an allowance and not a wage. Conversely, where the employee status is emphasised, remuneration is regarded as an appropriate reward for productivity in the job and learning is a secondary activity. This point is relevant to comparisons between the United Kingdom and West Germany where firms in the former have traditionally regarded youth workers as employees and not trainees.

AN OVERVIEW OF THE ECONOMICS OF TRAINING

This section draws on the themes developed in the preceding account to examine the training process in terms of the supply and demand for labour and the implications of human capital theory.

Supply and demand

A fundamental issue is the nature of the impact of training on supply and demand, whether it be training by individual firms using their own finances or government-sponsored training schemes. In this discussion it is assumed first that the demand and supply of labour schedules describe the conventional relationships between the wage rate and the level of employment and second, that training for skills in a particular market will have the effect of shifting to the right the labour supply curve. For analytical purposes two categories of market with wages below and above equilibrium are considered.

FIGURE 2.1 LABOUR MARKET WITH WAGES BELOW EQUILIBRIUM

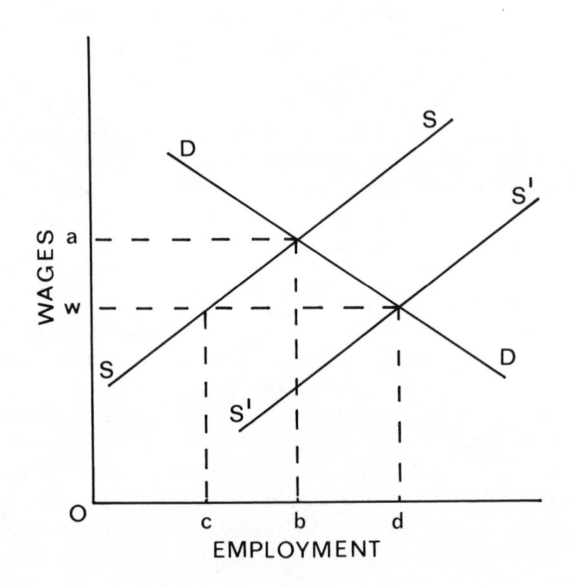

In both diagrams the equilibrium wage and level of employment is 0a and 0b respectively. In Figure 2.1 excess demand is cd, and the excess supply of labour is ef in Figure 2.2. In principle equilibrium can be restored by either adjusting the wage or shifting the demand and supply curves.

With a wage-adjustment policy the wage will rise from 0w to 0a and eliminate the labour shortage by reducing the quantity of labour demanded from 0d to 0b and expanding the quantity of labour supplied from 0c to 0b (Figure 2.1). The excess supply in Figure 2.2 can be removed by reducing the wage from 0w to 0a; the quantity of labour demanded will increase from 0e to 0b and the quantity of labour supplied will decrease from 0f to 0b. On the other hand if a supply-demand shift is initiated to restore equilibrium, a supply shift is generally likely to be appropriate where the wage is below equilibrium (SS to S'S' in Figure 2.1), and a demand shift is suitable where the wage is above the equilibrium level (DD to D'D' in Figure 2.2).

FIGURE 2.2 LABOUR MARKET WITH WAGES ABOVE EQUILIBRIUM

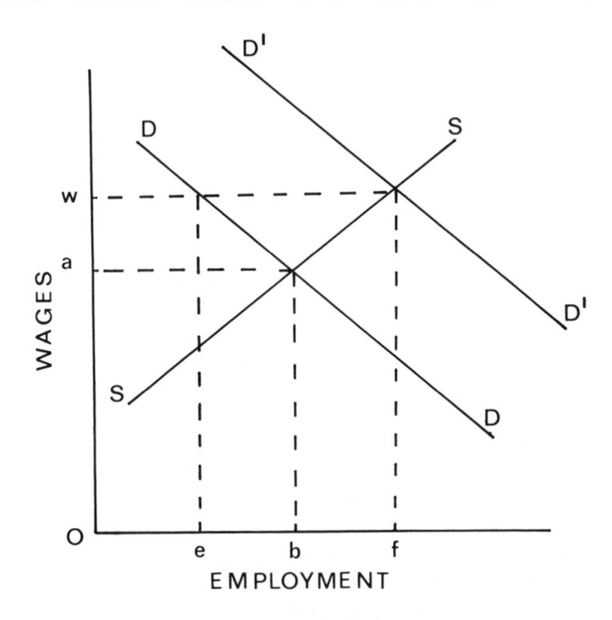

Arguably these cases are asymmetrical at the level of the individual labour market, because while it might be feasible to introduce policies to shift the supply curve for particular skills it might not be possible to shift the demand curve using conventional demand-management policies.

Whether or not wage-adjustment or a shift in supply and demand is more appropriate to restore equilibrium depends on the elasticities of demand and supply and the type of disequilibrium. If the price of labour is above its equilibrium level a fall in wages is likely to lead to a relatively large increase in employment if demand is relatively elastic, and a shift in demand is likely to lead to a relatively large increase in employment if supply is relatively elastic. If demand is relatively inelastic falling wages lead to a relatively small increase in the amount of employment and disequilibrium is eliminated by a substantial adjustment in wages. If wages are below their equilibrium level a rise in the price of labour has an expansionary effect on employment through the supply side of labour, and this will be larger the greater the elasticity of supply; and the increase in employment resulting from a shift in supply will be greater the higher the elasticity of demand.

The upshot of this discussion is that neither supply nor demand side policies are appropriate for correcting all cases of disequilibrium. If wages are above their equilibrium level either demand expansion or wage-adjustment will restore equilibrium, but the case for expanding the supply of labour is weak. In a multi-market economy there will be some markets with a potential for upward wage adjustment or an expansion in labour supply, but these markets will be exceptional in an economy with an overall excess supply of labour.

It is often suggested that youth wages in the United Kingdom are above their equilibrium level. One of the features of government policy is to seek to lower relative wages in the market for 18 to 20 year-olds by the operation of the New Workers Scheme, and this is consistent with the above analysis. However, current policy is also concerned with a lowering the equilibrium wage itself by shifting the supply curve to the right through the YTS. While some argue that these policies are diametrically opposed others maintain that they are mutually reinforcing in lowering wages in the youth labour market. However, whatever the view taken the analysis implies that employment will be greater and the underutilisation of human capital resources smaller if these policies are accompanied by an increase in demand.

Human capital theory and training policy

Human capital theory has three main implications for training policy. First, if firms rather than trainees bear the cost of general training and if this is not accompanied by a compulsory levy on all firms, there are potential benefits for companies undertaking less than their share of training if they are able to attract workers from other firms at the end of the training period. Second, learning-by-doing or on-the-job training is an essential part of the training process and some of the skills for particular occupations can only be gained at work. Where learning-by-doing is significant there is a weaker case for expecting employers to offer a low training wage because there is no reduction in productivity during training. Third, reliance on a market solution for the provision of economy-wide training is likely to lead to an underinvestment in skill provision both because the social rate of return will probably exceed the private rate of return and because of the existence of imperfect capital markets, particularly where the investment is in human rather than in physical capital.

3 Trends in youth training and unemployment

The recent trends in training in Great Britain can be generally described as an acceleration of a longer term decline and are summarised in Tables 3.1 and 3.2. Table 3.3 provides a longer term view of these trends and Tables 3.4 and 3.5 contain a breakdown by industry of apprentices and other trainees respectively for selected dates between 1970 and 1985. The numbers of apprentices as a percentage of all employees for EEC member countries in 1978 and 1981 are included in Tables 3.6 and 3.7. Unemployment rates by age in the United Kingdom and Great Britain are shown in Table 3.8 and unemployment duration by age in Great Britain is given in Table 3.9.

DEPARTMENT OF EMPLOYMENT DATA ON TRAINING

Information on the numbers of apprentices and other trainees in manufacturing industries in Great Britain has been collected by the Department of Employment since 1964. A sample of employers has been asked to submit the numbers of employees serving apprenticeships and the numbers undergoing other kinds of formal training. The sample has been stratified so that selection is proportional to size of establishment. There have been a number of changes through the years (Department of Employment, 1980, pp.946-947) but these are not seen as distorting the main trends of the data.

The annual numbers of apprentices and other trainees in manufacturing industry by sex for Great Britain from 1981-86 and the corresponding percentages of total employees are included in Tables 3.1 and 3.2 respectively. During this period the number of apprentices declined by 56.8 per cent from 147.6 to 63.7 thousand, and the number of other trainees fell by 39.3 per cent from 62.9 to 38.2 thousand. The proportionate decrease was greater for males in each case. These are substantial falls in such a short period and have resulted in a reduction in both apprentices and other trainees expressed as a percentage of total employees. It should be noted that the figures since 1983 may be distorted to some extent as generally they do not include YTS trainees. In some cases the YTS has been used as a first year for apprentice training, but these apprentices will generally be included in the figures only if they have a contract of employment and this is the exception rather than the rule.

This recent decline in training provision accentuates a trend which can be traced back at least to the early seventies. Table 3.3 summarises the extent of this decline for the 1970-85 period and shows that female apprenticeships as a percentage of employment are the only exception to the steady downward trend. Given the much lower proportion of apprenticeships for females this exception is little consolation for the general decline.

The numbers of apprentices and other trainees are also available by Industrial Order. The figures in Tables 3.4 and 3.5 show that no sector has exhibited any clear movement against the general trend. However, there were some exceptions between 1975 and 1980 where Chemicals and Allied Industries, Mechanical Engineering, Instrument Engineering, Electrical Engineering, Vehicles, Metal Goods and Other Manufacturing showed an increase in apprenticeships in both absolute and percentage terms, but where figures are available there were no exceptions between 1980 and 1985.

There are two points to note about these data. First, the figures for both apprentices and other trainees are restricted to the manufacturing sector, and it must be acknowledged that part of the decline is due to the response of employers and school leavers to the changes in the economy towards a larger service sector (Roberts, Dench and Richardson, 1986). However, the significant feature is the fact that the reduction in the numbers of apprentices and other trainees has been more rapid than the decline in the number of employees. For manufacturing industry as a whole the numbers of apprentices and other trainees expressed as percentages of the number of employees in Great Britain fell from 2.7 per cent to 1.4 per cent and 2.5 per cent to 0.7 per cent respectively between 1970 and 1985. Moreover this trend was reflected in all manufacturing industries for which data were available. It may well be that training provision has also fallen in the service sector of the economy, but comprehensive data are not available. Second, it is probable that many of the damaging economic consequences of this decline will only be realised in the long term. There may be a vicious circle of high unemployment, less training and low growth which the market economy cannot easily change given the short time horizon of many private firms.

EUROPEAN COMPARISONS

Training provision by the United Kingdom in relation to other EEC member states is summarised in Tables 3.6 and 3.7, but comparisons of this kind should be made cautiously given the changing nature of apprenticeship schemes throughout Europe. The United Kingdom was ranked fourth behind West Germany, the Republic of Ireland and Denmark for the number of apprentices as a percentage of all employees for all industries in both 1978 and 1981, and third behind West Germany and the Republic of Ireland for manufacturing industry. The United Kingdom figures range from 3.1 per cent to 3.7 per cent and are higher than the Department of Employment's figures (Tables 3.4 and 3.5) because the measurement of employees excludes apprentices and trainees and also is restricted to establishments employing more than ten persons.

It has been argued that the decline in the number of apprenticeships can be attributed to five main factors (Magnussen, 1979). First, the increase in demand for formal education has encouraged the substitution of costly apprenticeship schemes. Second, the increased mobility of labour and minimum wage laws have discouraged employers from training apprentices because the training costs are high and the returns cannot be guaranteed. Third, the wages of skilled workers have not always risen faster than unskilled workers. Fourth, rising wage costs have resulted in some substitution of capital for labour. Finally, there is a trade union fear that easier access to apprenticeship training and lower training allowances will undermine the adult wage rate. Many of these factors are likely to continue in the future.

The content of apprenticeship training has changed significantly in recent years. Broader occupational categories have been achieved by combining apprenticeable occupations to provide a more flexible training content where trainees can leave with intermediate qualifications and even re-enter at a later date. This process can be readily observed in the shift to "modular" training programmes and in the development of off-the-job training centres. One effect of the flexible approach has been a reduction in the time required for apprenticeship training. Advocates of this new form of apprenticeship argue that it provides for variations in the length of training to suit the requirements of individual companies and allows trainees to be assessed by achievement levels rather than by the amount of time served. Clearly this process must be balanced against the possibility of a reduction in the quality and extent of training.

The quality of apprenticeship training has been questioned especially in small- and medium-sized firms, and in many cases there is a tolerance of poor training in an attempt to expand and maintain training places. Another widely acknowledged criticism in some countries is the narrow specialisation of apprentice training, and while this leads to occupational immobility in for example Great Britain, it does not appear to be the case in West Germany.

Finally it must be acknowledged that the decline in apprentice training may in part be a welcome and realistic development. Roberts(1984) argues that apprenticeship training may be too costly and may lead firms to undertake training that is insufficient in quantity and inadequate in quality. However, the fall in apprentice training has a further implication for young people who experience no training of any kind. Employers may, with good reason, expect that these individuals will be harder to train in the future when new skills need to be acquired so that the prospects for the untrained school leaver may remain poor even if the demand for labour increases.

YOUTH UNEMPLOYMENT

One aspect of Government policy in the United Kingdom has been the pursuance of policies designed to restrict the increase in youth unemployment compared with the level of unemployment in other age groups. Unemployment rates prior to 1983 are not strictly comparable with more recent figures because of changes in the system of counting, and Table 3.8 indicates the changes that have occurred between 1983 and 1986. While the unemployment rates for all ages showed a slight rise over the period in both Great Britain and the United Kingdom, the unemployment rate for the under 18's has shown a downward trend for a major part of this time. Although a number of influences have probably been at work it is arguable that the option to school leavers of joining a training scheme is one explanation for the relative decrease in youth unemployment. However, the most recent figures suggest that this downward trend has at least been arrested and perhaps even reversed.

Unemployment Duration

The stock of unemployment at any time is equal to the duration of unemployment multiplied by the net flows into and out of that stock. Figures for unemployment duration by age for Great Britain between 1983 and 1986 are included in Table 3.9. It is apparent that over the period all of the designated age groups experienced a reduction in persons unemployed for between 27 and 52 weeks inclusive both in absolute terms and as a proportion in total unemployment. The main differences in duration experience between the age groups occur in the "0-26 weeks" and "over 52 weeks" categories. Generally and overall there was a decrease in persons below the age of 20 both in absolute terms and as a proportion in total unemployment in both duration classes, and an increase in persons over 19 years of age, particularly in the "over 52 weeks" category.

4 Industrial training policy in the United Kingdom

During the late 1950's and early 1960's there was much discussion about the inadequacies of both the quality and quantity of industrial training in the United Kingdom. To the extent that this contributed to low productivity and shortages of manpower it was considered to be an important factor underlying the low growth rate of the British economy. The facilities for and organisation of training were thought to be increasingly inadequate both in securing the appropriate skill mix in the supply of labour and in providing individuals with opportunities to adapt to technological change. An additional spur to action was the imminent increase in school leavers as a result of the post-war bulge.

THE INDUSTRIAL TRAINING ACT (1964)

This concern led to the passing of the Industrial Training Act of 1964. The main objectives had been set out in the White Paper "Industrial Training : Government Proposals" (Cmnd 1892, 1962), and were : "(i) to enable decisions on the scale of training to be better related to economic needs and technological developments; (ii) to improve the overall quality of industrial training and to establish minimum standards; and (iii) to enable the cost to be more fairly spread."

The Act might be said to have heralded a new era of Government intervention in the field of training. From the time of the first world war, the Minister of Labour had power to provide training courses for the unemployed and disabled. The Employment and Training Act of 1948 extended these powers by making it possible for the Minister to provide training courses for unskilled persons who were willing to take up a skilled trade, and employed persons who might be helped by training to achieve more regular employment.

The 1964 Act clearly built upon the 1948 Act, but it introduced the important new principle that all employers, regardless of whether they provided any training or not, had to contribute to a fund to be used for training purposes. There was a feeling that there was a need for "shock therapy" without imposing yet another burden upon management. The intention was to introduce a system which offered some form of rough justice. The idea was widely accepted because the natural reaction to the question of how to make industry train more was to make those who trained badly and those who simply "poached" do their fair share (Lindley, 1983). The proposals sought to manipulate the incentive/disincentive system rather than coerce employers into training their own manpower; employers were still at liberty to evade involvement in training, but they would now have some idea of the cost of this course of action.

Industrial training boards

The main vehicle for reform was the establishment of an industrial training board system. Industrial Training Boards(ITB's) were to operate a levy/grant scheme on their respective industries, by which a levy or payroll tax was imposed on all firms and grants would be paid out only to those firms achieving acceptable training standards and maintaining adequate numbers of trainees. Generally levies were between one and two per cent. The grants made by some boards covered the total cost of training, but other boards felt that grants which covered only an element of training costs were a sufficient stimulus. By 1972 there were 27 ITB's covering industries employing 15 million workers. Total income amounted to £208m and included grants of £5m from the Department of Employment. The training board initiative thus resulted largely in the collection and redistribution of money from firms with only modest supplementary financial assistance from the Government.

Criticisms of the 1964 Act

In contrast to a certain amount of general agreement before the introduction of the Act, there was subsequently considerable criticism. The criticisms fell into two distinct categories; some questioned the whole philosophy of the Act, while others accepted the underlying philosophy but pointed to weaknesses that became apparent during its operation.

The more fundamental criticisms of the principle of the Act were made by the Becker School of Human Capital Theory, (see Chapter Two) and they questioned the assumption underlying the Act that firms which did not train skilled workers were poaching. They argued that if the costs of general training were passed on to the employees in the form of lower earnings, labour mobility did not involve any loss to the firm which provided the training. Furthermore, they also pointed out that the approved standards which training schemes had to satisfy in order for firms to obtain repayment of the levy would result in an increase in general training at the expense of specific training and that these costs should be borne by trainees and not employers.

Although the Act was designed to increase both the quality and quantity of training, critics pointed out that it provided no additional funds for training, but merely attempted to reallocate resources within an industry (Lees and Chiplin, 1970). The implication was that the stick and carrot principle embodied in the levy/grant system may be self-defeating over time because as training standards were evened-up a board would come to collect the levy and then distribute it back again to the same firms having incurred the associated administrative expenses. This would bring about a once-and-for-all improvement in training standards but there was nothing built into the system to provide dynamic encouragement to industrial training. Johnson's suggestion of a subsidy or grant to the trainee would have provided additional funds and been consistent with the principles of general training (Johnson, 1971).

A further shortcoming of the ITB arrangements was that the once-and-for-all increase in training was being encouraged without any economic assessment of whether the additional investment in training by individual firms might have been put to more profitable use in other productive activities. The system tended to encourage training for the sake of training because as firms had to pay the levy in any case they had a strong incentive to incur training costs up to the level of the corresponding grant. The correct test was to equate the yield at the margin on resources invested in training with that in other uses. Markets will do this in at least a rough-and-ready way, but there was no such mechanism built into the training board set-up.

The training board structure was also criticised on the grounds that it was not designed to deal with problems of redeployment of labour across sectors and between local labour markets, because of the problems of co-ordinating a relatively large number of industry training bodies, each with different priorities framed to meet the needs of its own industry rather than those of the national economy or a local labour market. Thus a board could attempt to train workers who were in declining occupations in an industry, but the machinery could not cope with the problem of retraining workers in declining industries.

The second main category of criticisms of the ITB's was more concerned with practical weaknesses than with the fundamental objectives of the Act. The record keeping and paperwork necessitated by the levy/grant schemes were probably the greatest source of concern, and small firms in particular felt that many boards adopted too rigid an approach to assessing training needs. The Bolton Committee (1971) pointed out that many small firms did not qualify for ITB grants because their training was usually informal on-the-job training, whereas the boards emphasised the need for off-the-job training and gave high priority to the employment of full-time training officers, which may be inappropriate to small firms. On the other hand many boards such as Engineering provided exemption from the levy for the smallest firms (Department of Employment, 1968); some made provision to reduce the amount of paperwork for them while others encouraged the formation of group training schemes to enable them to benefit from economies of scale. The MSC reported that firms belonging to a group training scheme concluded that the scheme had an important influence on their training policy (MSC, 1980, para. 3.16) but that generally small firms ranked the influence of the ITB on training policies lower than did larger firms.

While the notion of making the poacher pay provided the original justification for the training board system, in practice the re-distribution of levy income to achieve this objective had become a secondary consideration by the time the Department of Employment carried out its review of the

ITB's in 1971-72 (Department of Employment, 1972). As the training boards developed they had become more concerned with the training activities of their constituent firms and had diversified their activities to include the training of managers, technicians and operatives. Grant schemes moved towards those which rewarded "the introduction and operation of a sound system of training in firms related to each firm's particular training needs" (Department of Employment, 1972, p.59). Firms with sound training schemes were exempt from the levy/grant scheme of certain boards (e.g. Petroleum) on condition that they paid a much smaller levy in order to contribute to their board's general costs and maintained regular contact with the board staff so that their progress could be monitored. The more the training boards moved in this direction, the less the likelihood that skill shortages would be reflected in the distribution of grant relative to levy.

THE EMPLOYMENT AND TRAINING ACT (1973)

The Government concluded from its review of the ITB's that the general levy/grant system had provided an initial "shock treatment" which had led to a major change in the attitude of industry to systematic training. However, while levy/grant schemes had never been relevant to the needs of small firms, there was now a serious risk that they were becoming an obstacle to the effective development of the ITB's, so that they should be phased out at a reasonably early date and replaced by more selective financial support. The outcome was the Employment and Training Act, 1973 which introduced a levy/grant exemption scheme. In effect this represented the second phase of a modification of the commitment to redistribution. The first had occurred quite soon after the establishment of the ITB system in 1967 when attempts to set levies at rates sufficient to cover the total costs of training were abandoned in the face of considerable opposition. There was a fear of an escalation in levy rates to pay for the training that would be stimulated by full cost reimbursement at a time when disparities between industries in the treatment of firms were already beginning to arise. The 1973 Act went further , however, by providing for Central Government financial support of the general operating costs of boards so that small firms and firms which trained workers "adequately" would be exempt entirely from the levy/grant system, and yet continue to use the advisory services of their board. Government financial support also made it possible to restrict the levy to a maximum of one per cent of payroll to meet the criticisms in some industries about the size of levy. The main purpose of levy exemption was to discourage paying firms to train more manpower than they required for their own purposes and charging the cost to other firms. Thus the emphasis had now shifted to making sure that all firms trained sufficiently if the overall training effort was to be maintained.

There were, however, several limitations on the capacity of levy exemptions to secure an adequate quantity of training in transferable skills to meet the needs of an industry or the economy as a whole. First, levy exemption under the Act depended on the adequacy of a firm's training arrangements. The emphasis was therefore on "arrangements" and not on the quality or quantity of training outputs. Second, levy exemption depended on the adequacy of those arrangements as measured against a firm's own needs, but predictions of the quantity of training which an individual firm required to meet its own needs would normally be subject to a certain margin of error. Even the most thorough planning system was likely to fail to take full account of changes in all of the factors which might affect training needs, particularly the demand for its products and its likely future profitability. Furthermore it is difficult through a system focusing on individual firms' needs to make adequate provision for the skilled labour needs of newly established firms that develop in a dynamic economy, not least when there is a sudden upsurge in the demand for products or services.

In its review of the 1973 Employment and Training Act the MSC concluded that while current training arrangements had made a major contribution to improving the quality of training, their effectiveness in stimulating appropriate levels of training had been limited, particularly in the area of transferable skills (MSC, 1980).

REFLECTIONS ON THE 1964 AND 1973 ACTS

The 1964 and 1973 Acts made two particularly important contributions to improving the quality of training. First, they introduced a greater professionalism into the assessment of training needs and the management and execution of training. This was achieved partly through an increase in the number of qualified training officers from 1,532 in 1965 to a peak of 3,436 in 1971 and 3,148 in 1978. Second, they helped secure more systematic learning through ITB's and other industry training organisations, through published recommendations and advisory work on training, and through encouraging or directly establishing facilities for full-time off-the-job training. This is reflected in the increasing proportions of first-year craft or technician apprentices in such industries as engineering, construction, shipbuilding, steel and road transport who receive training in off-the-job training establishments. For example in 1978-79 in engineering 90 per cent of the first-year craft or technician trainees reported to the ITB received off-the-job training as against 80 per cent in 1972/73 and 52 per cent in 1966-67.

On the other hand both the evidence from unions affiliated to the TUC and that from CBI members cast doubt on whether the arrangements introduced under the 1964 and 1973 Acts had been fully effective in influencing the quantity of training. However, unions affiliated to the TUC went further and specifically located the problem in the changes made in 1973. In their view the provisions on levy exemption, the one per cent upper limit on levy and the exclusion of small firms had placed substantial limitations on the ability of ITB's to provide more effective training arrangements within firms and on avoiding skilled manpower shortages within their industries. This was substantiated by research commissioned by MSC, although it did appear that a majority of firms preferred levy exemption because it involved less bureaucracy (MSC, 1980).

The changing labour market conditions of the 1970's provided a further stimulus for a thorough reassessment of the role of manpower policy. The 1964 and 1973 Acts had focussed on the need to tackle shortages of skilled workers rather than shortages of jobs for skilled workers. Policy was based on the sovereignty of demand to which supply was to respond more efficiently than had been the case in the past. The main instrument of policy was a financial one, but the administration of the system of ITB's provided a large degree of discretion over how this instrument was to be exercised. However, during the 1970's the labour market became increasingly characterised by a prolonged labour surplus rather than current shortages, and a reappraisal of policy was required (Lindley, 1980).

MORE RECENT DEVELOPMENTS

During the last ten years there have been several aspects to the development of manpower policy:

Special training measures (1975-79) constituted a counter-cyclical programme under which between 30,000 and 40,000 young people per annum in the United Kingdom were helped to obtain apprenticeships or other long term training. MSC funds were channelled through both ITB's and other industry training organisations.

Training for skills : a programme for action (TSPA) was a long term programme designed to maintain a consistent and permanent means to deal with training in important skills. From the financial year 1979-80 TSPA replaced the selective annual assistance provided under the special measures and other ad hoc programmes by what amounted to a permanent system of marginal funding.

Unified vocational preparation. From 1976 education departments and the MSC in conjunction with certain ITB's mounted an experimental programme of unified vocational preparation for employed young people to help meet concern about their training and vocational preparation in non-craft occupations. Existing programmes were transferred to Mode A schemes under the YTS in March 1983.

Youth Opportunities Programme (1978-83) contained within it elements of subsidy, work experience and training, and its introduction must be set against reductions in the Youth Employment Subsidy and Job Creation Programme. YOP was incorporated into the YTS in 1983.

Employment and Training Act, 1981

New Training Initiative, 1981

The Employment and Training Act, 1981 is discussed below. A review of the policy measures adopted in the youth labour market in Great Britain during the last ten years is included in Chapter Five, and the New Training Initiative is examined in Chapter Six.

EMPLOYMENT AND TRAINING ACT (1981)

Outlook on Training (MSC, 1980) concluded that the solution to the problem of local and cross-sector needs lay with the existing statutory framework and not in the dismantling of the present organisational apparatus in the belief that firms could be relied upon to adopt forward-looking training strategies. The approach of influencing training through industry-focused training organisations has a number of advantages such as decentralisation and the ability to respond quickly and flexibly to perceived problems. Also responsibility for determining the level of resources to be secured from firms in order to meet the needs of their industry rests with the representatives of both sides of that industry.

The review did, however, give rise to certain specific proposals which indicated the direction in which the ITB system was likely to move. It was recommended that industry should once again be responsible for the funding of the ITB operating costs except where an ITB agreed to act in effect as an agent of the MSC in pursuance of a priority national objective.

This proposal to make industry more responsible for financing and providing training was reflected in the Employment and Training Act, 1981. However, the Act went considerably further in this direction than had been suggested in Outlook on Training. The economic philosophy of the Conservative Government clearly predisposed it to closing the ITB's down altogether leaving those industries that wished to retain their boards on a voluntary basis to make their own arrangements. The Act cleared the ground for the abolition of the boards after consultation with but no longer on the recommendation of the MSC. The number of ITB's has subsequently been reduced from twenty-four to eight at the present time, covering agriculture, construction, engineering, clothing, hotel and catering, road transport, rubber and plastics, and offshore petroleum activities.

In the remaining ITB's (or any authorities that replaced them) the Act sought to change the basis of funding by returning the operating costs of ITB's to the firms in the industries they serve unless they are located in enterprise zones. The argument appears to be that the absence of levies and bureaucratic interference will provide a stimulus for firms to set up in enterprise zones, while other firms will demand a greater say and more efficiency in the running of boards if they have to pay for their administrative costs (Dutton, 1982). However, the additional burden of an increased training levy is not something that British industry is happy to take on board at the present time. The economic situation has worsened considerably since firms were freed from paying for the administration of ITB's in 1973.

The implication of the 1981 Act is that the monitoring of training needs within an industry is jeopardised where ITB's have been disbanded or when a significant number of firms within an industry are exempt from contributing to running costs or from supplying employment statistics. It cannot be deduced that small firms will not train, but as no one will know whether or not they are training it will make life difficult for other firms in the industries concerned, and make estimates of the supply and demand of trained labour in industries as a whole subject to wide margins of error.

5 Special employment and training measures, 1975-1986

While manpower policy has been dominated by the debate about industrial training for the last two decades, the seventies were characterised by a rapid diversification in a number of measures designed to generate employment and encourage training. In the eighties these develcpments were scaled up to become major factors in the employment and training of all age groups but especially young school leavers. The present discussion is restricted to an appraisal of those employment and training measures which have had and are having a bearing on young people in Great Britain. The inclusion of measures designed primarily to stimulate employment is justified on the grounds they offer work experience and also that they are often accompanied by training of some sort (see Chapter Two).

Table 5.2 shows the numbers of people in Great Britain between 1975 and 1986 covered by those special employment and training measures which have had some bearing on young workers. Several trends can be identified. First, there has been a substantial increase in the numbers involved during the period. The average quarterly numbers supported rose from 18.4 thousand in 1975-76 to 259.6 thousand in 1985-86. Second, there has been a movement away from market-related measures which are designed to reduce the level of unemployment through altering the costs of recruiting, employing and training, and towards a broad programme creating opportunities for the young unemployed outside the labour market. Third, and more recently, there has been a shift in emphasis away from the problem of youth unemployment and towards the question of youth training with the setting up of the YTS.

The measures outlined in Tables 5.1,5.2 and 5.3 can be grouped in the following way for analytical purposes:

(a) Wage subsidies (Recruitment Subsidy for School Leavers, Youth Employment Subsidy, Young Workers Scheme and New Workers Scheme).

(b) Community Industry.

(c) Training in Industry (Special Training Measures).

(d) Training for Skills : A Programme for Action.

(e) Unified Vocational Preparation.

(f) Work Creation Programmes (Work Experience Programme, Job Creation Programme and the Youth Opportunities Programme).

WAGE SUBSIDIES

Wage subsidies can be paid either in relation to the numbers recruited (flow) or the numbers employed (stock). If the subsidy is to the stock, it can be paid in relation to the total numbers employed (general) or to some change in the numbers employed (marginal). Furthermore the subsidy can be flat-rate or varied in relation to characteristics such as age or region.

In general there is a stronger case for a marginal stock subsidy than for a recruitment subsidy. While the former takes account of both inflows to and outflows from the stock of employment, the latter could result in little increase in employment with a substantial budgetary cost if the outflow from the stock of employment is high.

A marginal job subsidy also has advantages over a general subsidy. An arrangement whereby the subsidy is confined to the extra jobs provided as a result of the subsidy means that a given expenditure will generate many more jobs than the same expenditure spread over all workers particularly in an open economy. In a closed economy the effect of any subsidy on domestic demand is somewhat limited. Taking wages as given, all subsidies have their effect mainly by reducing prices, and prices cannot fall below the average cost of the marginal firm. Since the price elasticity of aggregate domestic demand is low (Layard and Nickell, 1980) the effect on demand will probably be relatively small. However, in an open economy with exports and import-substitutes matters are quite different, and a marginal subsidy can have a much bigger effect on employment than an average subsidy costing the same amount. Since exports and import-substitutes will rise, the balance of payments is likely to improve, and since the same expenditure generates more jobs this way than if it were spent on general reflation, the budget deficit is much less adversely affected. In fact an ideal marginal job subsidy would pay for itself if the saving on unemployment benefit plus additional taxes paid exceeded the subsidy.

The Recruitment Subsidy for School Leavers

However, the history of subsidies in Great Britain shows a preference for recruitment subsidies in the youth labour market. The Recruitment Subsidy for School Leavers (RSSL) was introduced in October 1975 and paid out £5.00 a week for 26 weeks to any employer who recruited an unemployed school leaver who had never worked or worked for under six weeks. In its evaluation of the Scheme the Department of Employment concluded that the subsidy had very little effect in terms of the additional recruitment it brought about. In replies to a survey 76 per cent of firms claiming the subsidy stated that they would have recruited as many school leavers in the absence of the subsidy. There was little evidence of the displacement of other young people working full-time on a permanent basis, but 14 per cent of firms reported that they had substituted school leavers for part-time adult females and temporary workers (Department of Employment, 1977b).

The Youth Employment Subsidy

In the light of this evidence it was decided to concentrate special help on the least advantaged in the age group and RSSL was replaced in October 1976 by another recruitment subsidy limited to those who had been unemployed for over six months, though available to all young people under 20 years old rather than school leavers only. This Youth Employment Subsidy (YES) was worth £10.00 per week for up to 26 weeks for each eligible young person recruited for full-time work. The average quarterly numbers supported in Great Britain reached a peak of 8.5 thousand in 1977-78 (Table 5.2) but the Scheme was subsequently run down in the transition to the Youth Opportunities Programme which is discussed below. Surveys conducted by the Department of Employment suggested that subsidised workers did not tend to be employed only in unskilled jobs and that they were as productive as other young workers. There is also evidence that the subsidy had an effect in "launching" young people into permanent full-time employment. However, the effect on recruitment was very similar to that under RSSL, and employers reported that 75 per cent of the subsidised young people would have entered their employment regardless of the subsidy (Department of Employment, 1978b). The effect on total employment is difficult to compute because employers were only asked about the impact of the subsidies on the flows into their employment rather than the effect on the stock of workers employed. In addition displacement and multiplier effects should also be taken into account. The small size of the employment effect substantiates the point that subsidies to flows are likely to be less effective than marginal stock subsidies.

The New Workers Scheme

The New Workers Scheme (NWS) is the only subsidy for young people currently in operation. Introduced in April 1986, the subsidy is designed to promote the recruitment of young people to jobs with relatively low pay and, at the same time, to induce employers to keep pay low enough to be able to obtain the subsidy. This reflects the view that youth unemployment is higher than it might be because in Great Britain the wages of young people are relatively high proportions of the adult rates. Employers receive a £15 a week subsidy for a year for every 18-and 19-year-old that they employ at wages of £55 a week or less and for every 20 year-old that they employ at wages of £65 a week or less.

The Young Workers Scheme

The NWS is based on the same principles as the former Young Workers Scheme (YWS) which it replaced. Between its introduction in January 1982 and March 1986 employers made 436.7 thousand successful applications to the Scheme in Great Britain. A recent evaluation of the YWS has been concerned with the extent to which it reduced the numbers of unemployed young persons and the associated cost to Government funds (Bushell, 1986).

The analysis distinguishes between deadweight, substitution, induced jobs and displacement. Deadweight is the extent to which expenditure on the YWS finances the employment of young workers who would have been employed anyway, and is estimated to have been 63 per cent of the numbers supported. Substitution is the extent to which expenditure on the YWS results in the employment of otherwise unemployed young people but at the expense of those who would have been in employment in the absence of that expenditure, and was about ten per cent. Young workers in induced jobs comprised 27 per cent of the numbers supported; these are the jobs that would not have existed in the absence of the Scheme. Displacement is the most difficult to measure, and is defined by Bushell as the extent to which expenditure on the YWS assists output among employers entitled to claim support, but at the expense of those who are unable to make use of the Scheme. The cost advantage for recipients might lead to a loss of output and employment among non-recipients and thereby reduce the overall effectiveness of the Scheme in providing new jobs. However, there was evidence that the increase in output attributable to YWS support was small in relation to turnover. Also, it was not possible to find any consistent link between those establishments claiming output effects and those indicating that the YWS had enabled them to create induced jobs.

The net cost per person no longer unemployed as a result of the YWS was estimated to be £1400 per annum at 1985-86 prices. This represents a fall over time which was due to a rise in the number of jobs induced by the Scheme since 1982-83 .

COMMUNITY INDUSTRY

The Community Industry Scheme (CI) was established in 1972 and is run under the auspices of the National Association of Youth Clubs (NAYC). It is funded by a Government grant which is administered by the MSC.

CI aims to help socially and personally disadvantaged young people prepare for permanent employment by providing them with practical work of benefit to the community. Participants, most of whom are aged 16-17 are employed in small work teams on environmental improvement and other projects, and in workshops. Scotland has been relatively successful in monitoring projects under this Scheme and has had a consistently high share of places in Great Britain (averaging over 20 per cent in recent years). The average quarterly numbers supported in Great Britain reached a maximum of 7.0 thousand in 1982-83 and 1983-84 (Table 5.2).

TRAINING IN INDUSTRY

Through its ongoing discussions with ITB's and other training organisations the Department of Employment has been able to exert an indirect influence on intakes of apprentices and other trainees. In recent years, however, the MSC has had more direct means of influence, and from 1974-79, as part of Government counter-recession policies, operated a programme of "Special Measures" in collaboration with ITB's and certain training bodies in the non-Board sector. The three main objectives of the programme were:

(i) to safeguard long term economic interests by making good any shortfall in the level of entry to long term training occupations

(ii) to help ensure that there is an adequately trained labour force ready for economic recovery, and

(iii) to help preserve training facilities that would be needed again in the near future.

The Training in Industry programme(TI) consisted of two main groups of measures. First, measures for influencing intakes in order to meet future shortfalls in the supply of skilled manpower and second, measures designed to safeguard the continuity of an individual's training (e.g. Adoption Grants). There were two main measures for influencing intakes; per capita Premium Grants were designed to encourage employers to recruit young people for long term training in areas of agreed intake "norms", while Training Awards provided first-year training and associated further education under ITB sponsorship for young people without an employer, where the Board anticipated a shortfall in recruitment by employers relative to its industry's long term needs. The average quarterly numbers supported by these schemes in Great Britain reached a peak of 28.7 thousand in 1977-78(Table 5.2).

A case is sometimes argued for introducing countercyclical training programmes in a recession because the opportunity cost is low due to the relatively high levels of unemployment. Although there is some resource cost in terms of the reduction in utility due to the leisure foregone, there is no cost in terms of foregone production. On the other hand it is arguable that there is a case for tackling the problem from the demand side and stimulating the economy through tax cuts, especially if the stimulus can be diverted to those parts of the economy which are suffering relatively severely from a temporary downturn. Not only will this be less inflationary than demand directed to those parts of the economy which are more stretched, but there are major efficiency gains from maintaining the structure of productive activity rather than breaking up patterns of work, provided this is justified in the long run (Layard, 1979).

With the recession continuing and deepening the Special Measures Programme began to develop into a semi-permanent labour market feature, and it became desirable to seek an alternative method of funding additional intakes if future skill shortages were to be minimised. This aspect was included in a wider review of training for vital skills carried out in 1977, and from 1979-80 the various schemes were subsumed into a permanent Training for Skills Programme(TSPA).

TRAINING FOR SKILLS : A PROGRAMME FOR ACTION

TSPA contained proposals for a long term programme to improve the quality and quantity of training in skills needed by industry, to discourage a "stop-go" attitude to training and to help prevent persistent shortages in skills from building up. While cyclical fluctuations are important in creating medium term imbalances in the number of people entering transferable skill occupations, the nature of skills in demand and the overall balance of the various skills which make up the labour force, while affected by cyclical factors, are more likely to be influenced by the process of structural change in industry. This would include the secular decline and expansion of particular sectors, as well as technological developments. These changes may be less obvious than cyclical fluctuations, but unperceived needs in new skills in rapid transformation can lead to permanent labour market problems. It was to these long term structural imbalances that the TSPA programme was directed. An important feature was its arrangements for dealing with skill shortages common to several industries. In an attempt to meet some of the criticisms levelled at the 1964 and 1973 Acts, the MSC became responsible for bringing together ITB's and other organisations when imbalances in cross-sector skills were identified.

Amongst the criteria by which the TSPA programme was operated were guidelines intended to foster fundamental changes in attitude towards entry to training in industry and its basic organisation. These guidelines were that all training should lead to agreed standards; that the lengths of craft and technical training should be related to what has to be taught and to the rate of learning of the individual, with incentives to qualify as quickly as possible; and that opportunities should be available for the later acquisition or updating of skills. For example the Engineering Industry Training Board has been building up a Craft Module system since the late 1960's but these developments are the exception rather than the rule.

The transition from Special Measures to Training For Skills criteria for supporting industrial training was intended to be gradual in order to give industry time to adjust to the new arrangements. ITB's and other training organisations were being asked to improve their manpower planning, to accept more responsibility for their full training commitments and to initiate the introduction of training standards. However, these aspirations were partially thwarted by the deepening recession, and some counter-cyclical help for industry continued for a longer period than had been originally planned.

UNIFIED VOCATIONAL PREPARATION

A pilot programme of Unified Vocational Preparation (UVP) schemes was launched in July 1976 for an initial period of three years. The programme was subsequently extended and incorporated into the YTS in 1983. The available data is more comprehensive for Scotland where the target population was the group of young people of about 20,000 annually who leave school with minimal or no formal qualifications and enter employment where they are unlikely to receive any systematic training or further education. If there is no obvious skill content in the traditional sense employers are not likely to look for opportunities to release youngsters for further education. An initial scepticism amongst employers meant that the pilot programme got off to a slow start (Table 5.1) but subsequently they have received some benefit from an improvement in the maturity of outlook and approach to work of their trainees and a reduction in labour turnover.

In some ways UVP offered a training similar to that in the Youth Opportunities Programme which is discussed below. In both cases the emphasis was on general skills by transmitting broad skills as well as those of the particular industry involved, and putting work in its social environment. UVP was designed to help young people think realistically about themselves and their futures, to develop basic skills, understand society, and strengthen the foundations of skill and knowledge on which further training could be built.

Training took place partly in the employer's premises and partly in further education colleges on block- or day-release courses and lasted about 13 weeks. Two-thirds of them were sponsored by ITB's, and the remainder by firms and colleges of further education. In the 1980-81 financial year the cost of schemes varied from £2,400 for catering assistants to £9,400 for construction operators, and the average cost per trainee was £408. More than half the total of Scottish UVP courses were sponsored by the Distribution ITB, but the total programme was very small and by March 1981 this had amounted to only 652 trainees in schemes involving that Board. This is a particularly disappointing record when compared with German experience where a great many of the 450 or so apprenticship schemes in the Federal Republic are to be compared not with traditional United Kingdom craft training but more readily with some form of UVP.

YOUTH OPPORTUNITIES PROGRAMME

In October 1976 the MSC appointed a working party to study the feasibility of putting into effect an objective of ensuring that all those between the ages of 16 and 18 who had left school and were not engaged in full-time education and were unable to get a job should have the opportunity of training or of participating in programmes such as the Job Creation and Work Experience Programmes. The Holland Report, Young People and Work (MSC, 1977) reviewed the problem of youth unemployment, evaluated the various measures that had attempted to deal with it and proposed a new structure of provision which, with few modifications, was to become the Youth Opportunities Programme (YOP) in April 1978.

The Job Creation Programme

The Job Creation Programme (JCP) had been introduced in October 1975 to provide worthwhile temporary jobs for those who would otherwise have been unemployed. Initial emphasis was placed on the 16-24 and over 50 age groups, but the Work Experience Programme (WEP) took over the responsibility for 16-18 year-olds from the JCP in September 1976, and this in turn was subsequently absorbed into YOP.

Although the JCP had links with CI's thinking and experience it had much more in common with the Canadian Local Industries Programmes. The JCP provided funds for sponsors (mainly local authorities and to a lesser extent voluntary bodies) to run short term projects lasting not more than a year, and on average 32 weeks. They were labour intensive, with the programme only paying wages at the normal rate plus ten per cent towards running costs. In 1976 about one-third of the projects were for environmental improvement, a sixth were construction projects, a third were social service or educational and the rest were mainly concerned with research and surveys.

There are major problems in evaluating the JCP mainly because of the lack of information about the costs and effects of the Scheme. The evaluation published in the Employment Gazette (Department of Employment, 1977a) is descriptive rather than analytical and no mention is made of, for example, the possible effects of displacement on the employment of other people. However, the Scheme has been fairly heavily criticised. First, there has been doubt as to the value of the projects' outputs. To many people it seemed strange that at a time when local authorities were having to cut back on activities that they valued, they were encouraged to initiate less valued projects that were required by the Programme to be "new". This problem is intrinsic to the nature of selective measures, but of course it may well be compatible with other objectives. The second main criticism concerned the Scheme's lack of success in providing a bridge to permanent employment. Only between six and seven per cent of participants transferred to their sponsor's permanent workforce after the project was over, and two or more months after the project 47 per cent were out of work, most of whom had never worked since the project. Perhaps this was to be expected given the temporary nature of the projects and the programme was subsequently modified under the WEP.

The Work Experience Programme

The WEP was designed to provide young people with the experience of work without becoming a regular employee. Young unemployed people were paid £18 a week by the Government and attached to an employer for about 25 weeks.

They were placed by the Employment Services Agency with willing private employers, who were paid nothing but had an extra pair of hands around the place.

The WEP was generally more successful than the JCP in improving the employment prospects of its participants because it was embedded in the normal structure of working life. The evaluations published in the Employment Gazette (Department of Employment, 1978a) reported that 38 per cent of trainees stayed on with the same employer and 23 per cent had moved immediately to a full-time job.

Criticisms of The Youth Opportunities Programme

The Holland Report drew attention to a number of limitations inherent in the then existing measures that had attempted to deal with the problems of youth unemployment and training. For example the introduction of schemes on a temporary basis inhibited planning and development; the schemes had been introduced piecemeal with the result that there was little opportunity for progression between schemes; wages and allowances varied between schemes; there were relatively fewer opportunities for girls than boys; and there was no mechanism by which the experience and expertise acquired by people running schemes in the past could be made available to others. The Holland proposals aimed to meet some of these shortcomings by bringing the existing types of provisions within a co-ordinated programme.

The total number of YOP entrants in Great Britain increased from 162.0 thousand in 1978-79 to 553.0 thousand in 1981-82 (Table 5.3). The schemes fell into two broad categories: work preparation schemes and work experience schemes. The work preparation schemes included employment induction courses, short training courses and remedial courses, and were designed to improve young people's capability in basic social skills and to focus their interests and aptitudes in a positive way to help them find and retain a job. The work experience schemes used different kinds of on-the-job work experience as a major medium of training, and included work experience on employers premises (WEEP), project-based work experience, training workshops and community service.

The former piecemeal arrangements had now been replaced by an informal hierarchy of schemes corresponding to the needs and abilities of the young people concerned. At the top was WEEP which offered work experience amounting to broad vocational preparation in an actual work-place and under supervision. On the other hand young people with lower educational attainments tended to derive more benefit from project-based work experience or community service.

However, the principle of the 'ladder of opportunity' was particularly difficult to implement, partly because of the pressure of numbers and partly in view of the number of separate bodies involved in YOP. In evidence submitted to the Select Committee(Committee on Scottish Affairs,1981-82), it was reported that of those who entered YOP in September-October 1979 only nine per cent of those in Scotland had gone to another MSC scheme while 29 per cent were registered unemployed. The figure for progression from short training courses was much higher at 26 per cent partly because of special Scottish initiatives to deal with this, but the overall pattern of improvements was nevertheless very patchy.

However, by 1981 there was growing concern over other aspects of YOP and criticism was beginning to be focussed on four main areas. First, the size of the allowances payable to trainees; second, the use of trainees as substitutes for other labour; third, the low average quality of education on the programme; and fourth, the falling placement rates of YOP graduates.

In 1981 the weekly allowance paid to YOP trainees was held at £23.50 for a second year with no adjustment for inflation. The YOP trainees who most resented the low allowance argued that as they were doing the same work as many ordinary employees who were earning two or three times as much they should be paid accordingly. The feeling that trainees were being exploited as "cheap labour" was quite common on some of the employer-based WEEP schemes, and is linked to the second criticism of substitution.

The principal concern was that some employers took on YOP trainees instead of having full-time employees. The employer might have employed a succession of trainees to avoid a new hiring, and instead of paying wages he engaged trainees whose allowances were paid by the taxpayer. Not only was this practice undertaken at the taxpayers' expense, but it was also unfair to the trainee who would have gained little from the experience. From evidence submitted to the Select Committee(Committee on Scottish Affairs,1981-82) it was estimated that in Great Britain all work experience schemes taken together probably had a substitution rate of about 20 per cent, and WEEP a rate of between 20 and 30 per cent. However, it is arguable that these figures might have underestimated the extent of substitution since they were collected on the basis of approaches to employers (Youthaid, 1981). On the other hand the Scottish figures might have been somewhat lower because MSC monitoring was more frequent in Scotland.

A third criticism levelled against YOP was the allegedly low average quality of education and training on the programme. The strongest criticism was directed at the WEEP schemes where it was alleged that pressure of numbers resulted in the MSC pursuing quantity at the expense of quality, and many trainees did not receive the variety of occupational experiences that the programme was intended to offer. In a wide-ranging review of off-the-job training on YOP it was reported that in 1981 only 28 per cent of work experience trainees were offered off-the-job education or training (Greaves, Gostyn and Bonsall, 1982).

YOP was also criticised for its lack of success in terms of the placement rate of young people who had been through the Scheme. The placement rate in Scotland had fallen steadily. Of those who entered in September-October 1978 only 13 per cent registered as unemployed at the end of the Scheme, while the corresponding figure for entrants in January and March-April 1980 was 48 per cent. The YOP schemes with the best subsequent employment rates tended to be the WEEP schemes with the worst record of education and training. This was partly due to the opportunity WEEP gave an employer to scrutinize a youngster with a view to offering him a permanent job, and also to the tendency for better qualified young people to enter WEEP.

Apart from its immediate effect on the unemployment register, most of the effects of YOP on the labour market came about through its effects on the demand side of the market even though it was designed to intervene on the supply side (Raffe, 1984). The programme was the victim of changing economic circumstances, and the deepening recession was a fact of life that any new initiative that might be taken would have to face.

6 The Youth Training Scheme

THE NEW TRAINING INITIATIVE

The New Training Initiative was launched by the MSC in May 1981 with the publication of A New Training Initiative : A Consultative Document. It stated general objectives rather than detailed proposals, and three inter-related objectives were outlined:

(i) the development of skill training including apprenticeship in such a way as to enable young people entering at different ages and with different educational attainments to acquire agreed standards of skill appropriate to the jobs available and to provide them with a basis for progression through further learning.

(ii) a move towards a position where all young people under the age of 18 have the opportunity either of continuing in full-time education or of entering training or a period of planned work experience combining work-related training and education.

(iii) the opening up of widespread opportunities for adults, whether employed, unemployed or returning to work, to acquire, increase or update their skills and knowledge during the course of their working lives (MSC,1981a,para. 23).

The document argues that the compelling need is for a training system which enables all workers to acquire a basic range of skills and to develop and adapt them throughout their working lives to take advantage of the rapidly changing requirements of markets and technology. The training of young people provides the foundation for what should be a continuous process throughout the individual's working life, and should be viewed in a longer term context than has often been the case in the United Kingdom. In the past employers have too often taken or been forced by financial problems to take the short term view of regarding training as a dispensable overhead rather than an investment for the future.

The long term approach to training implies that employers and trade unions need to jointly determine the range of skills and knowledge to be covered and the level of performance required, and to embody these in "standards" which individuals will recognise and accept. This in turn will probably lead to a gradual phasing-out of time-served apprenticeships. Such bodies as the City and Guilds of London Institute, and the Scottish Vocational Education Council(SCOTVEC) can make a valuable professional contribution in the area of testing standards of individual competence.

The Consultative Document argued that the cost of achieving the objectives should be shared between employers, employees and the Government. Employers will benefit from having a more adaptable workforce capable of more rapid development and change. Individuals will benefit from a wider range of skills, increased capability and therefore less vulnerability to change. The country will stand to gain the net benefit from improved industrial performance and hence increased wealth. It seems reasonable therefore to expect these beneficiaries to contribute to the costs.

However, the main responsibility for tackling the problem of training should rest with employers (and their representative bodies) and trade unions, with the Government and the MSC playing a supportive role. There is scope for supporting each of the three objectives : the first through an approach by the MSC to the Government for the provision of funds to increase the number of grants offered for full year apprentice training where it is satisfied that all appropriate measures have been taken or are planned by industries to maintain adequate training levels; the second by the development of the existing YOP and UVP to provide experience and a foundation on which provision for all young people under 18 years of age can eventually be built; and the third by the widening of opportunities open to adults by concentrating increasingly the Training Opportunities Scheme on key skills which are in greatest demand.

An agenda for action

The MSC received nearly one thousand written submissions on its Consultative Document. The main points were summarised in the document A New Training Initiative : An Agenda for Action (MSC,1981b)and the comments received showed overwhelming support for the three objectives. Although Agenda for Action made few specific proposals it echoed the earlier themes of the importance of standards and the need to adopt a long term approach to training. It argued that it may well be in the interests of the community that in future individuals are trained beyond the needs of a specific job and for a range of skills. As firms and individuals cannot be expected to invest in training to meet needs which they may not recognise or which offer no prospect of early returns, new means of public funding must be devised which recognise the public and private benefits of training and the need for substantial State involvement. It proposed to establish a "high level task group" to include the CBI, TUC, education interests and others to consider these issues and report by April 1982. This was to become known as the Youth Task Group(YTG).

A programme for action

The debate was transformed by the Government White Paper A New Training Initiative : A Programme for Action (MSC,1982a) which was published at the same time as An Agenda for Action. It proposed to replace YOP with a new and better youth training scheme which would effectively integrate skills, knowledge and experience through planned and supervised work experience and properly designed opportunities for off-the-job training or further education, and would provide for induction, assessment, guidance and counselling.

However, some aspects of the White Paper's proposals were strongly criticised. First, the proposal that the guarantee of a full year's foundation training should be restricted to unemployed 16 year-old school leavers was contrary to the Consultative Document's second objective and to the submissions received in response. Second, the White Paper's proposals to set the allowance payable to unemployed 16 year-olds at "around £750 a year" and to remove their eligibility for supplementary benefit in their own right threatened to alienate trade unions, potential trainees and employers. Although the proposed YTS allowance was intended mainly to cover travel and other expenses it still compared unfavourably with the (then) YOP allowance of £1,300 per annum. The removal of entitlement to supplementary benefit was to be offset by a continuation in the payment of child benefit to the parents and justified on the grounds that trainees are in a similar position to those who choose to go on at that age to further education. This corresponds closely to the West German view of youth training. However, both the reduced allowance and the element of compulsion implicit in the supplementary benefit proposals threatened to discourage participation by unions, trainees and employers who had no wish to become involved with unwilling recruits.

The Youth Task Group

The YTG reported in April 1982 (MSC, 1982b). The broad outlines of its proposals were accepted by the Government two months later, and were to become the basis of the YTS.

As Raffe has pointed out, "At first glance the YTG performed a financial miracle" (Raffe, 1984). The YTG was well aware that the Government's policy of further reducing spending meant that the cost of any alternative plan had to be kept within the £1,000 million cost of the White Paper's proposals, and yet the YTS was to be expanded from 300,000 to 460,000 trainees a year, and the allowance raised from £750 to up to £1,450 per annum. The key to this "financial miracle" lay in what has come to be known as the "principle of additionality", according to which each employer was expected to take on three additional trainees for every two young people normally recruited in order to qualify for a grant in respect of any young trainees. With the level of allowance in the region of £1450 the Task Group proposed that the grant should be £1950 per annum for employer-based schemes. Thus the proposals were financially attractive to many employers, who would consequently not have to pay the wages of their first year trainees, would get a contribution towards their training costs and also would have the productive services of the additional YTS trainees.

THE YOUTH TRAINING SCHEME

The YTS came fully into operation in September 1983. The aims of the Scheme are:

(a) to provide all young people participating in the Scheme with a better start in working and adult life through an integrated programme of training, education and work experience, which can include work in and for the community, and a record of achievement, which can serve as a foundation for subsequent employment or continued training or relevant further education;

(b) to provide for the participating employer a better equipped young workforce which has acquired some competence and practical experience in a range of related jobs or skills, thus enabling him to operate more productively in an increasingly competitive trading environment and in a period of often rapid and far-reaching technological and market changes; and

(c) to develop and maintain a more versatile, readily adaptable, highly motivated and productive workforce which will assist Britain to compete successfully in the 1980's and beyond.

Scheme modes

In its original format three months of each placement consisted of off-the-job training and education which could be at further education colleges or training centres. For the remaining nine months trainees were placed with firms for on-the-job training. Placements were either on Mode A or Mode B schemes. Mode A were schemes where an employer, Chamber of Commerce or industrial training organisation agreed with the MSC to act as a managing agent and arrange a complete programme of work experience, training and education. The agent either provided a complete YTS programme or subcontracted out all or some of the elements such as on-the-job training. Mode A schemes were open to both employed and unemployed young people and the managing agent received a fee of £100 and a block grant of £1,950 for each trainee as a contribution towards training costs including the trainee's allowance.

On Mode B schemes the MSC acted as the managing agent and only unemployed young people were eligible. A distinction was made between B1 and B2 schemes. Under Mode B1 the MSC arranged with one sponsor (such as a local authority or voluntary organisation) to provide a complete programme for the individual in a Training Workshop, Community Project or Information and Technology Centre(ITeC). Once-and-for-all capital grants were available, and agreed expenditure including staff salaries, operating costs and trainee allowances were reimbursed within defined limits. The Mode B2 or "linked" schemes were primarily a reversal of the Mode A pattern, and were built round a short course of off-the-job training and education supplemented by work experience or placements with one or more employers.

There were important differences between Modes in terms of cost, relative size and provision by sector. First, the annual cost of a filled place was higher for Mode B than Mode A schemes, and higher for B1 schemes than for B2 schemes. In 1984-85 the estimated annual cost was £3,800 for Mode B1 schemes compared with £2,300 for B2 and £2,050 for Mode A schemes. And within Mode B1, ITeC's were most expensive at £4,300 per filled place, Training Workshops cost £4,000 and Community Projects were £3,550. Because of the overhead component the cost differential between Modes A and B for unfilled places was larger than that for filled places and about £2,000 per place per annum. Second, almost three quarters (73.0 per cent) of entrants to the YTS in 1984-85 in Great Britain were in Mode A, and 22.8 per cent were in Mode B1, Community Projects accounted for 14.6 per cent and ITeC's for only 1.7 per cent (Table 6.1). The complementarity of Modes was particularly apparent at the regional level. Arguably it was more difficult to provide places on Mode A schemes in regions experiencing relatively depressed levels of economic activity and it might be hypothesised that there is an inverse relationship between the proportion of trainees in Mode A schemes and the regional unemployment rate. Figures for 1984-85 support this hypothesis (Table 6.2) , and the rank correlation coefficient between the proportion of YTS entrants into Mode A for 1984-85 and the average unemployment rate was -0.845.

There were also differences between Modes in their provision by sector. Almost two thirds of schemes and 60 per cent of places were being provided by employers and other organisations in the private sector in October 1983. More detailed analysis shows that the private sector and private training agencies were providing almost three quarters of the Mode A places and that the public sector and voluntary organisations were providing more than 80 per cent of the places on Mode B schemes.

Skill and learning classifications

The MSC recognised from the beginning that achieving high quality schemes would be a major challenge and issued general guidance on designing schemes round eight "design elements" and six "learning opportunities". Thus all schemes in 1983-84 were designed to include an induction period, occupationally based training and planned work experience together with a minimum period of 13 weeks off-the-job training. Guidance and support for trainees was required throughout the year, aided by the establishment of regular assessment, review and recording of progress including the issue of a leaving certificate to all trainees.

Managing agents were also required to provide training in five "core areas" of learning namely: numeracy and its application, communication, problem solving and planning, practical skills and computer literacy and information technology. Each scheme had to offer opportunities to learn about the world of work and the world outside employment, including trainees' interaction with the community. There had to be an opportunity to develop as a worker and as an adult in terms of inter-personal skills and self-organisation, and schemes had to provide trainees with the opportunity to acquire job specific skills relevant to their placements, and also a broad range of skills that they could transfer in different social and work settings. Skills are grouped around a common "key purpose" to form OTF's (Table 6.3). They are designed to provide a means for organising training rather than offer a comprehensive occupational classification.

THE INITIAL DEVELOPMENT OF THE YOUTH TRAINING SCHEME

While the general principles of the YTS were enunciated by the YTG, many of the details were left unspecified so that the working model was rather the product of a continuous evolutionary process. The issues are varied and controversial, and may be discussed against a background of the tendency to pursue the quantity of places at the expense of quality in 1983-84, and to aim for consolidation thereafter.

Planned and approved places

Regional data on the number of places on the YTS and the number of entrants to the Scheme have been published monthly in the Employment Gazette since July 1983. A distinction was made between planned places and approved places. The number of planned places is based on assumption by the MSC on the number of 16 and 17 year-olds likely to enter the labour market, the proportion likely to find employment and the proportion who will be unemployed, and the number of young people in employers' normal intakes of school leavers who will be brought within the scope of the YTS. It was also necessary to make assumptions about the number of young people who will leave further education or employment during their first year and thus require the balance of a year's training on the YTS. The MSC took the view that the maximum number of places it could afford and fill in 1983-84 in Great Britain was 459,770 (Table 6.4).

Approved places are those that have been negotiated between sponsors or managing agents and the Area Offices of the Training Division of MSC, and have been considered and agreed by MSC Area Manpower Boards. Also included are schemes that have been negotiated centrally by the Large Companies Unit, accepted by Training Division Area Offices and approved by the Youth Training Board.

The approval of schemes ,assistance with monitoring, and assessment are all functions of 56 Area Manpower Boards, who also have a vital role in co-ordinating and overseeing the local development of the YTS. They succeeded a network of 29 Special Programmes Area Boards and 88 District Manpower Committees in April 1983. The Chairman is independent, and each Board includes local representatives of employers, employees, local authorities, educational interests and voluntary organisations. Principal Careers Officers are not members, but have the right of attendance for discussions on youth training.

To ensure that large companies play their full part in the YTS a Large Companies Unit was set up. It dealt with 20 per cent of Mode A places in 1984-85 and dispenses with the need for companies to have to go over the same ground many times with different area offices.

The Youth Training Board representing employers, trade unions, local authorities and education and voluntary organisations was set up at national level to oversee the whole Scheme. It is assisted by the Advisory Group on Content and Standards.

Concessions to employers

The early months of the YTS were characterised by a series of concessions to reduce employers' obligations and thereby encourage them to join the Scheme. First, it was agreed that existing training programmes would be acceptable for the YTS as long as they included at least three months off-the-job training and irrespective of whether they met the other conditions. Second, the intention of requiring that YTS projects be linked to broad occupational requirements was dropped in the face of employers' resistance, particularly in the construction industry. The industry has been allowed to run a scheme which sets out to train young people for specific jobs and so abandoning the idea of a broad-based training that would prepare them for a variety of occupations. According to the Chairman of the Construction Industry Training Board (CITB), "The builder does not want the MSC's idea of a general handyman, expensively trained by the taxpayer, turning up on site and giving the services of a Jack or a Jill of all trades and master of none" (Times Educational Supplement, 6 January 1984). The CITB is in a strong bargaining position, managing the YTS training for the whole industry, running training schemes at its own centres and in 1983-84 having succeeded in filling 17,296 of its 21,000 places. Third, some employers were allowed to break away from the YTS concept that actual work should provide the bulk of the foundation year. For example a scheme to use the YTS to train most of the entrants into engineering apprenticeships was approved by the MSC. Engineering employers were encouraged to take on about 40,000 school leavers in 1983 of whom about two-thirds were likely to be earmarked as apprentices, and they were able to claim the YTS grant for all of them. In engineering young people start by taking a first unit of off-the-job training, after which those who are not selected for apprenticeships gain further work experience. The apprentices then either go on to a second module followed by three months on-the-job training, or spend the whole year off the job as has been the case in the past. Both groups of apprentices are trained to the standards of the Engineering Industry Training Board's first year certificate. This amounts to a departure in principle by the MSC, even though those apprentices who spend the whole year off the job are still trained according to the YTS criteria.

Apprentices and the Youth Training Scheme

The MSC aimed to encourage training to standards without

regard to age as the basis of its funding of apprenticeships from 1984-85, and the YTS minimum criteria are of critical importance in providing a foundation on which young people can build. Where the general expectation is that young people will progress directly from the YTS year to subsequent stages of skill training the MSC has indicated that YTS support will be forthcoming so long as the overall package of training, including periods beyond the YTS year, is consistent with the YTS minimum criteria. On the other hand, where schemes covering the initial year of an apprenticeship or other long duration training do not include a clear expectation of continual training, the first year itself should comply with the minimum criteria. In schemes like Engineering where there is a delay in identifying trainees who are to be retained as apprentices, the critical factor in funding is the contribution that the YTS training will make to the prospects of those people who are unable to continue with the apprentice training programme (Youth Training News, No. 10, April 1984).

Commercial training companies

The provision of a sufficient number of Mode A places was also assisted by the arrival on the scene of several commercial training companies specialising in clerical and retail skills. The incursion happened because the companies believed that as managing agents they could at least break even on the YTS projects and possibly even run them at a profit. This was a possibility that had not originally been taken seriously by the MSC because the assumption from the start had been that Mode A managing agents would be mainly employers who would need to spend more than they received in grant, and that this would be offset by the value of the work performed by the trainees. The implication was that these companies could only hope to break even if they kept down training costs or levied a charge on sponsors or reduced administration costs by operating on a large scale. Levying a charge is now the rule rather than the exception, and is discussed more fully in Chapter Seven. Most training companies are well aware of the need to avoid the criticism that they are undercutting other products by marketing cheap and subsidised goods. This version of the cheap labour argument centres on the elasticity of substitution between workshop and non-workshop goods rather than the more usual version which focuses on the elasticity of factor substitution between YTS trainees and other manpower. Sponsors are able to avoid the charges of unfair competition by concentrating on a product mix whose elasticity of substitution with other goods is zero.

Monitoring

While the emphasis in the first year had been on the development of an effective structure for delivering the Scheme, the second year was a period of consolidation. An important part of this process was an increase in the contribution made by MSC staff to the effectiveness of YTS programmes by better targeted and more closely-focused monitoring. It was recognised that YTS monitoring was increasingly about promoting successful practice among those running the YTS rather than merely preventing abuse.

The central intitiative from the MSC's Quality and Standards Branch was the production of a Revised Design Framework. The original Design Framework had been widely criticised because of a certain amount of duplication among the design elements and learning opportunities, and because the distinction between the inputs and outputs of the Scheme was unclear. The Revised Design Framework formed the basis of the Design Framework for the two-year YTS (Chart 6.1).

THE TWO YEAR SCHEME

The third year of the YTS (1985-86) was a period of planning for the two-year Scheme that became operational in April 1986. The purpose of the extended Scheme is the provision of a training programme leading to vocational qualifications with at least 20 weeks off-the-job training over two years in addition to a planned programme of on-the-job training and work experience. It offers two years training for 16 year-old school leavers and one year for 17 year-old leavers. It provides for a training agreement between the trainee and those responsible for his or her training setting out their respective responsibilities and rights, including details of each young person's training programme. From April 1987 only approved training organisations will be able to take part, and a new Training Scheme Advisory Service will be set up to maintain the quality of the training provided.

Funding

A major change in the general funding arrangements is the abolition of the distinction between Modes with all schemes now financed on the basis of a per capita block grant. There are two components: first, a management fee of £110 per contracted place that is payable at the start of each of the two years of the programme; and second, a basic grant of

£160 per calendar month that is payable on filled places for up to 24 months.

In certain cases a premium grant of £110 per calendar month is also payable for up to 24 months on filled places. This is intended to meet the needs of young people who require initial work experience away from the pressures of a commercial environment, and also to provide training in areas where employer-based places are insufficient. The combination of basic and premium funding is designed to meet the circumstances of the average premium place provider when the two-year Scheme is fully established. In its calculations the MSC has assumed an 85 per cent level of occupancy, a 2:1 ratio of first to second year places and also that second year trainees are in work experience placements in which employers will be generally expected to contribute to training costs. The MSC has also recognised that some schemes might face transitional problems, and has made available funding for these purposes in 1986-87 and 1987-88. Allocations of up to a maximum of £70 per filled place per month will be made to schemes whose current average unit costs are higher than the unit costs incurred in 1984-85.

Allowances

On the cost side trainees receive a higher allowance in their second year. This can be justified on several grounds such as the need to provide encouragement and motivation, the desirability for payments to increase with age and the fact that trainees are more productive and therefore worth more to the company in their second year. On the other hand there is the constraint that the second year allowance should not encroach upon the wages paid to first year apprentices and other low paid junior staff in the organisation. First year trainees are currently paid £27.30 a week and second year trainees receive £35.00 per week. The implication of this is that when fees for college-based courses are also taken into account the Scheme has been underfunded by the Government and must rely on financial support from employers.

Approved Training Organisations

The MSC regards the development of Approved Training Organisations (ATO's) as the single most important factor in establishing the credibility and quality of the Scheme. In the majority of cases the ATO will be a managing agent, but whatever the nature of the organisation the essential point is that it has unity of management with responsibility for decisions about its programmes so that it can effectively offer two-year YTS. ATO's must satisfy the MSC on ten criteria including their previous record in training, the resources of the organisation and financial viability, the competence of staff and suitability of premises and equipment, and a positive commitment to health and safety and providing equal opportunities. In return the MSC will offer an extended three year contract to be rolled forward annually and thereby reduce much of the uncertainty that accompanied the previous arrangement of annual contracts. The MSC has also indicated that its subsequent monitoring activities will be less time-consuming for organisations and more concerned with trainee progress than organisational details since the ATO approval process will have already documented the latter.

Criticisms of the new scheme

The extension of the YTS to two years has received wide support from all sides of industry, and is generally regarded as a major improvement in the opportunities for training and work experience for young people. There are a number of economic implications for both employers and the economy as a whole and these are discussed in Chapter Seven. However, there are two reservations arising from the speed with which the consultation process was carried out, there being little more than three months between the announcement of the decision in the Budget speech in March 1985 and the Government's approval of the MSC's proposals in July. First, it is to be hoped that the first few months of the new arrangements will not be characterised by a series of minor modifications to rules and regulations. Of course not all difficulties can be anticipated in advance, but it is a question of balance and many employers are likely to be irritated by numerous adjustments. Second, the value of the Scheme is diminished if the second year amounts to little more than a duplication of the first year's programme. A number of employers in Dundee and Renfrew who were providing on-the-job training in clerical and retail related areas stressed that nine months was more than sufficient for training in these skills at this level, and it is questionable whether the consultation period offered enough time to produce a coherent training programme.

7 Appraisal of the Youth Training Scheme

EMPLOYERS' VIEWS OF THE YOUTH TRAINING SCHEME

There is a general consensus that the speed with which the YTS has been introduced is remarkable. The period since April 1983 has witnessed the development of a complex organisational network and the acceptance of a commitment to the YTS by many of the individuals and agencies involved with it, and this is reflected in a number of favourable responses from the surveys. For example in 1984 two-thirds of those employers with previous experience of other training schemes felt that the YTS was better than its predecessors. And in 1985 six out of seven employers were at least as optimistic about the Scheme as when it began; three quarters said that they were "very willing" to participate in an extended two-year YTS, and only one in ten said that they had had enough and did not want anything more to do with it.

It is critically important for the future of the YTS that the goodwill shown by employers should be harnessed, because the MSC in unable to operate effectively in a vacuum and must rely on the co-operation of the community as a whole if it is to perform successfully many of its functions. However, increasingly there is a danger of this goodwill being undermined by the direction in which the Government's training policy is moving in the prevailing economic climate. The warning bells have already been sounded in the general comments provided by employers. Many were highly critical of the size of the trainees' allowance and what they regarded as a general under-funding of the Scheme by the Government, while for others the impending changes in the funding arrangements for the two-year YTS were a source of considerable uncertainty.

THE MARKET STRATEGY

Recent Government training policy has been heavily influenced by its view that, as with the rest of the economy, the labour market functions most efficiently along free market lines. Examples of this strategy are the abolition of 16 Industrial Training Boards since 1981, the Consultative Document on Training in November 1984, the Government's declared policy of asking employers to bear an increasing proportion of training costs of the YTS and the abolition of the distinction between Modes in the YTS from April 1986. A common theme underlying all these initiatives is the self-improvement of individual decision making units within the economy, whether companies or trainees. The necessary and sufficient conditions if investment in training is to go ahead are a positive net present value in excess of the estimated returns on alternative investment projects. One implication of this policy is the emergence of a widening spread in the distribution of human capital and a dichotomisation of the youth labour market. The economic reasons underlying this have been discussed in Chapter Two.

MODE B SCHEMES

The abolition of the distinction between Modes has serious implications for the former Mode B Schemes. These schemes recognised the difficulty of providing places on demand for special needs groups, and often catered for many of the "less advantaged" young people. They would employ staff with a commitment to helping the young with their particular disadvantages with a view to making them acceptable for Mode A schemes in the longer term. However, since April 1986 the fixed costs of these schemes are no longer guaranteed. Funding is based on trainee occupancy, so that if a trainee leaves (for whatever reason including progress to employment or other training) all grants attached to that trainee cease forthwith and are not reinstated until a replacement is found. The extent to which alternative finance can be raised by charging placement providers or by charging for the goods and services provided is limited. Most external providers used by voluntary organisations are also community-based or charitable, and charging for goods and services will deny their services to the disadvantaged groups and people which the schemes have served in the past. Arguably the general thrust of present policies is very clearly in the direction of what Disraeli called "Two Nations".

EMPLOYER-FUNDING WITH A FALLING RATE OF RETURN

In addition to lowering the relative cost of community-based schemes present policies are also designed to reduce the proportion of the costs borne by the Government for all schemes. The 1985 survey found that some employers were already contributing to the cost of the YTS on a voluntary basis, but the funding arrangements for 1986-87 imply that all employers will be expected to contribute between £10 and £15 per trainee per week in addition to anything they might have contributed before if managing agents are to break even.

However, there are serious reservations about the current policy of shifting the balance of funding towards employers, particularly in the current economic conditions. The main concern is based on the arguments that many firms are unable to finance their own training at the present time, and also that high and continuing levels of unemployment are likely to reduce the rate of return or any investment that is made. In the course of the surveys a number of respondents stressed that there were some companies that were financially unable to support an increase in their training commitment at the present time, and they pointed out that the overall coverage would be uneven if training were left to the market mechanism. There is also the further point that general skills are likely to be more readily available in the market place in times of recession so there will be less need for firms to undertake this sort of investment.

There are two additional factors currently reducing the rate of return on the employer's training investment . The first is the voluntary nature of employers' involvement with the YTS and the second is the occupational distribution of YTS placements.

THE VOLUNTARY PRINCIPLE

There is a large measure of support for the principle that employer participation in the YTS should be voluntary, but there is a major problem in accommodating both the voluntary principle and the Government's intention that employers should eventually bear the major cost of vocational training. To the extent that this type of training is general and therefore transferable between jobs and companies, any employer who participates in the Scheme voluntarily and at his own expense is likely to be subsidising those employers who choose not to get involved, and arguably the poaching of skilled manpower could eventually undermine the whole basis of the YTS.

THE OCCUPATIONAL STRUCTURE

The second factor that is likely to reduce employers' rates of return on the training investment is the occupational structure of the YTS. A significant feature of the Scheme is a concentration of approved places in Clerical and Administration, Personal Services and Sales, Installation Maintenance and Repair, and Manufacturing and Assembly. And in 1984-85 for Great Britain 73 per cent of entrants into Mode A schemes were in these four OTF's. Moreover 45 per cent of entrants were divided equally between the Clerical and Administrative and Personal Services and Sales OTF's(Table 6.1). This pattern has tended to be stable from year to year and is reflected regionally throughout Great Britain. However, it is probable that there will be relatively small variations around the norm at the local labour market level.

The reversal of supply and demand

It is likely that this pattern of distribution is the result of pressures operating on both demand and supply. It is usual for the Careers Service to ask young people for their first and second preferences for training, and for the Area Manpower Board to approve suitable placements in the light of both this and the general industrial structure of the area. Trainees may prefer clerical and retail-related skills because on-the-job training in them is associated with relatively pleasant working conditions, and because trainees believe that these placements probably offer the best prospects for a job at the end of the YTS.

Supply-side forces are likely to become increasingly

important with the passage of time. The presence of several commercial training companies which entered the stage in the first year of the YTS means that the occupational structure of places has become partly institutionalised, and it is conceivable that increasingly the preferences of trainees will be conditioned by the availability of places in the clerical and retailing areas in particular.

The problems that this scenario creates for an integrated system of training should not be underestimated because it amounts to a reversal of the roles of supply and demand. Instead of the supply of trainable labour being matched against the demand for skills by employers, the demand for training places by young people is being matched against the supply of training places by employers.

Clerical and retail skills

There are serious reservations about the large number of trainees in retailing- and clerical-related skills. One concerns the apparent isolation from foreign competition of retailing in particular, while the other concerns doubts about the continuing ability of the economy to absorb many with either type of skill into full-time employment.

In the first place one of the main reasons behind the New Training Initiative(MSC, 1981a) was to make the United Kingdom's exports more competitive, but it is difficult to see how the benefits from training in retailing can make more than a minimal impact, if any, on the country's international competitiveness. It is not as though these "graduates" can transfer to sectors that are more export-related. Despite the intention that vocational training should be broad-based in character, there is evidence of skill specificity in the eyes of participating employers. For example in the 1984 survey half the employers said that their cost savings would be "very substantial" if they employed their own trainees, compared with 15 per cent if they employed a trainee from elsewhere. The 1985 survey showed that only 9 of the 144 (6.2 per cent) trainees offered full-time employment on completion of training in 1984 and 3 out of 86 (3.5 per cent) in 1985 had undertaken their on-the-job training with other employers.

Part-time employment

Reservations on the continuing ability of the economy to absorb successive outflows from the YTS into full-time employment are based on the growth of part-time employment in retailing and personal services and also on both the actual and potential substitution of capital for labour in clerical occupations. These features in particular are likely to lead to a reduction in the return on the training investment to employers.

The increasing use of part-time labour in retailing and personal services has been one way of raising labour productivity. It provides a means of adjusting labour capacity to reflect daily, weekly and seasonal peaks in demand and so contain wage costs. This diversity in working schedules has attracted increasing numbers of women to work for less than a full-time week and often at unconventional hours. For example, in June 1985 the proportion of female employees who were part-time was 61.7 per cent in Retail Distribution and 37.4 per cent in Personal Services. Furthermore in both sectors the number of part-time females exceeded the total number of male employees.

There are two features of this pattern which have a bearing on the full-time employment of YTS "graduates". First, there is evidence from a number of studies that the large number of part-time jobs in certain sectors is due to the pattern of employers' labour requirements and not to the need to meet a shortage in the supply of full-time workers (Robinson, 1985). Thus the problem for the young people completing YTS courses in retailing and personal services is that the jobs are part-time but the trainees are not. Second, it is normal practice for the occupational grading of staff to be more favourable to full-time workers than to part-time employees (Robinson and Wallace, 1984). This is so for a number of reasons including the preferential treatment of full-time workers in promotion policies and the employment of part-timers on work requiring lower skills. Thus it is arguable that many of the "graduates" from the Personal Services and Sales OTF who obtain jobs are likely to be trained to a level in excess of requirements.

New technology

Most discussion of new office technology currently focuses on the applications of microcomputers, and forecasts of the employment impact of information technology are very sensitive to the assumptions made about its rate of diffusion and the course of demand for such services. To date, developments in most economic sectors have resulted in increasing roles for office work, and in the short and medium term this trend may well continue with the reorganisation of production processes with new technology, and work systems. But as Gershuny and Miles (1983) have argued, "... there seems little reason to anticipate any surge in demand on a scale equivalent to the potential improvement in productivity associated with office technology" (P. 152). Williams (1984) has also concluded that increasing automation is likely to reduce the demand for clerical and routine secretarial tasks and may lead to some deskilling of the work of junior secretaries and typists. The changing composition of occupations and skills in services could have an adverse effect on female employment, given their concentration in clerical and secretarial work, unless they can develop a broader range of skills.

THE SOCIAL RATE OF RETURN

The rate of return on the training investment to society as a whole is also likely to be reduced by the current economic recession, at least in the immediate future. In the first place the skills of the people who are unable to obtain jobs on completion of the YTS will depreciate, and these people will become less suitable as recruits to employers the longer they are out of work. The results of the first large-scale survey on the destinations of young people completing the YTS in Great Britain were published in the Employment Gazette (Department of Employment,1984). It reported that 56 per cent of YTS "graduates" entered full-time employment, and implied that just under 30 per cent of the trainees became unemployed. This is generally consistent with the findings of the Dundee-Renfrew study that the ratio of job offers to trainees was just over 50 per cent at the end of the first intake in 1984.

LABOUR DISPLACEMENT

The second factor moderating the social rate of return on training is labour displacement. The point is that the training of young people in skills that are already available in the labour market represents a waste of scarce resources.

The concept can be adapted in a number of ways. For example, a distinction can be made between simple displacement and multiple displacement. Simple displacement occurs when the employment of a trainee displaces one other worker, and multiple displacement occurs when the simple displacement initiates a chain reaction of further displacement. And again, a more refined definition of displacement focuses specifically on the duration component, and takes into account the length of time by which a worker's unemployment is extended as a result of the displacement.

As employers could not be expected to furnish information on either multiple displacement or the duration of displacement, the main focus of this part of the enquiry centred on the number of persons directly displaced. It covered both the extent to which YTS trainees displaced other members of the labour force during training and the extent to which YTS-certificated young people displaced other persons on completion of their training. For analytical purposes three types of trainee were distinguished. First, trainees occupying jobs that had been vacant. Second, trainees occupying jobs that had been especially created for them. And third, trainees occupying "composite" jobs that combined elements of the first two categories.

One estimate of the trainee displacement rate was obtained by expressing the number of vacancies filled by YTS trainees that also could have been filled by non-YTS labour as a percentage of the total number of YTS trainees recruited into vacant jobs. For Dundee and Renfrew this amounted to over 90 per cent in 1984 and in 1985. Put another way this means that 18 per cent of the total number of trainees in 1984 and four per cent of the total in 1985 occupied vacant jobs that also could have been filled by people from elsewhere.

An alternative approach is to assume that trainees occupying jobs especially created for the YTS involve non-displacement, and to estimate displacement as a residual. The corollary is that trainees occupying "composite" jobs are involved in displacement rather than non-displacement, and qualitative information from the questionnaire returns shows this often to be the case. Displacement rates of over 50 per cent were recorded for 1984 and 1985 in Dundee and Renfrew by this method. Further evidence of a positive displacement rate is provided by Sako and Dore(1986) who found that one in twelve employers were using YTS trainees instead of older workers and the Committee on Scottish Affairs(1981-82) estimated displacement in pre-YTS schemes to be between 20 and 30 per cent.

Labour displacement by young people who had completed their YTS training was also relatively high. The returns showed that 74.0 per cent of the trainees in Dundee and Renfrew accepting the offer of a job in 1984 (and 65.0 per cent in 1985) took up vacant positions that could also have been filled by persons from outwith the YTS. In other words, just over one third of the trainees in 1984 displaced other workers from full-time jobs on completion of their training. This is comparable to a combination of the "deadweight" and "displacement" effects discussed in the appraisal of the Young Workers Scheme (Bushell,1986).

An assessment was also undertaken of the incidence of displacement for different occupational groups, and is relevant to the extent that training alleviates any skill shortages or replicates skills which are readily available in the labour market. In this case displacement was measured by the difference between the total number of trainees and the number occupying especially created jobs expressed as a percentage of the total number of trainees. The evidence suggests a relatively high displacement effect by young people who had completed their training in the Clerical (88.6 per cent) and Installation, Maintenance and Repair (55.2 per cent) OTF's in 1984. For the 1985 sample Installation, Maintenance and Repair (82.6 per cent), Personal Services (80.0 per cent) and Clerical (61.8 per cent) OTF's exhibit significant displacement. However, it should be stressed that the exercise was severely limited by the sample size and that it is hazardous to draw any firm conclusions.

By way of qualification there are two potential sources of error in the estimation of displacement effects from questionnaire returns. First, it is possible that employers may underestimate displacement, particularly where they may feel that an admission that trainees undertake the work of regular employees is inappropriate for a government-sponsored scheme. There is a natural reluctance to admit the possibility of using trainees as "cheap labour" and it is conceivable some employers may deliberately conceal the abuse of the YTS as a means of providing cheap labour services. Second, even if the information collected is provided in good faith, it is possible that employers are unable to measure accurately even direct displacement effects. Employers may have little or uncertain information on displacement because it requires a judgement of either future employment patterns or the hypothetical employment of alternative labour.

Government policy and displacement

Arguably one effect of recent Government policy initiatives has been to increase the level of displacement. The Young Workers Scheme had been introduced in January 1982 to promote the recruitment of young people to jobs with relatively low pay and from April 1984 had offered employers a subsidy of £15 per week for 17 year-olds in their first year of employment if they were earning £50 or less a week. Since April 1986 the scheme has been known as the New Workers Scheme, and eligibility has been extended to 18-20 year-olds. The point is that where subsidies like this are targeted on particular groups of workers without any corresponding increase in vacancies, labour displacement is likely to occur.

COSTS AND BENEFITS OF TRAINING

Any estimation of the rate of return on training presupposes some knowledge of the costs of and benefits from the investment, but a common response in both surveys was the problem of quantification. Many employers were able to suggest that trainees were either of little or great benefit or cost to their companies, but had no formal accounting procedures for verifying their views. However, returns from about 40 per cent of the sample suggest that there was an average positive benefit of about £200 per trainee per annum in 1985.

Whether the Government's declared intention that employers should bear an increasing proportion of the cost of the YTS over the next three years is matched by a corresponding increase in real benefits will depend critically on such factors as the proportions of trainees offered jobs, the rate at which these employees subsequently leave the company and the time period under consideration. However, in the immediate future firms will be faced with a continuous flow of trainees through the YTS without being able to recoup some of the longer term benefits from training, and it is unlikely that the real increase in costs will be matched by any real increase in benefits that might occur.

Topping-up of allowances

The most reliable figures on costs related to the practice of topping-up trainees' allowances. One in ten respondents were topping-up allowances for 27 per cent of the trainees. The practice tended to be confined to the medium-to-large organisations, and only two respondents employed less than 50 persons. The average amount of topping-up was £5.10 per week, but the range of individual cases was in excess of £25.00. The effect of this was to raise the average payment to all trainees by about five per cent. For Great Britain as a whole about 16 per cent of trainees received an additional payment which resulted in an increase of about seven per cent in the average payment to all trainees (Department of Employment, 1985). Some respondents saw topping-up as a means of attracting a higher calibre of trainee or more generally of overcoming the problem of unfilled places. Others argued that it was right that some trainees should be paid more than the basic allowance, particularly if they were making a contribution to the profitability of the company or if they were doing the same work as others who were being paid more.

However, just under one half of respondents believed that topping-up had adverse effects on the allocation of trainees between employers and on the trainees' morale. It is conceivable that the company paying the most would tend to attract the cream of the trainees. This would put pressure on companies which could not afford to pay more, and they would be faced with a choice of either reducing their numbers of staff or of withdrawing from the Scheme altogether. This practice could also cause unrest among the trainees, particularly when they compare notes during periods of off-the-job training. For the Scheme as a whole the problems could be intensified as multi-branch participants attempt to adopt internally consistent policies across different geographical areas. These problems were generally expressed by employers in the form of reservations, but six respondents were totally opposed to the practice of "topping-up".

THE LEVEL OF ALLOWANCES AND EMPLOYMENT

For many employers these problems would be mitigated if the trainees' basic allowance was higher. The size of the allowance was of major concern to many employers, and in their general comments on the Scheme 45 per cent offered quite spontaneously the view that the allowance was too low. They believed that the higher allowance would help to improve the attitude of those trainees who were in the YTS only under sufferance. There was no doubt that the general unwillingness of some trainees was a major constraint for a number of employers who felt that more willing participation on the part of the trainees would improve the Scheme considerably. Few employers were prepared to suggest a figure but a first year allowance of £35.00 per week was mentioned by several respondents as being "about right". There was also strong support from employers that trainees should receive a higher allowance in their second year than in their first and 85.5 per cent said that they believed it to be fair and reasonable.

THE WASTAGE RATE

One of the more controversial areas of the YTS has been the wastage rate of trainees, and discussion has focussed on both its size and its interpretation.

The controversy surrounding its size is due largely to the relatively obtuse way in which it has come to be measured. The problem arises because measurement is usually done at a particular point in time and comparisons are made between studies of different durations. A more satisfactory approach is to construct survivor functions for estimating the rate at which the trainees leave the YTS over time. The returns from the Dundee-Renfrew sample show that in 1984-85 15.4 per cent of the 263 trainees had left the YTS after 48 weeks. However, a sizeable proportion of this wastage occurred within the first two months, and 9.9 per cent had left the Scheme after eight weeks (Table 7.1). It is noteworthy that almost all the female wastage occurred in the first six to eight weeks after joining the Scheme. Of the trainees whose destinations were known to employers, approximately equal numbers took up full-time employment, joined another YTS scheme or became unemployed.

The drop-out rate receives attention because it has come to be regarded by many as an indication of the success or otherwise of the Scheme, the implication being that the premature departure of trainees is synonymous with incomplete training and a waste of scarce resources. However, this is an oversimplification, and individual cases should be judged on their own merits and take into account the occupational nature of the scheme, the length of time the trainees have been on it and their destinations on leaving. For example given the view expressed by some employers that a training programme in excess of about nine months is unnecessary in the clerical and retailing areas, a trainee leaving one of these schemes after nine months to take up a full-time job would be likely to impose a lower cost on society than say, an engineering trainee leaving after ten months and becoming unemployed.

RELATIVE WAGES AND EMPLOYMENT

It is often suggested that youth employment is strongly influenced by the relationship between youth and adult wage rates. It has been argued that in the United Kingdom the relative wages of young people are substantially higher than in other European countries particularly West Germany (Jones, 1982), that relative wages have been rising over many years and that such rises can be linked with increases in youth unemployment relative to the overall level of unemployment.

A number of studies have examined the relationship between relative wages and youth unemployment including Makeham (1980), Layard (1982), Lynch and Richardson (1982), Wells (1983), Hutchinson, Barr and Drobny (1984), Lynch (1984), Main (1985) and Rice (1986). There is no definitive conclusion on the matter, and the results vary according to such factors as the time period studied, the specification of the estimating equations and the choice of estimation technique.

While earlier studies tended to employ regression analysis more recent analyses have adopted a maximum likelihood technique. For example Lynch and Richardson (1982) used United Kingdom data for 1950-78 to regress the youth - total unemployment rate ratio on a number of independent variables, and found that the relative employment cost variable was significant. Furthermore there is evidence that the relative wage became more unfavourable during the seventies. On the other hand Main (1985) used a likelihood model to examine the extent to which the probability of employment is affected by various personal characteristics mainly relating to family circumstances, educational qualifications, the local unemployment rate and whether young persons had been on YOP. The interesting finding from the point of view of youth training is that YOP gave some advantage to school leavers compared with unemployed school leavers who were not on the Scheme, although the effect was less pronounced for males than females. In quantitative terms being on a YOP scheme increased the employment probability by five per cent for males and 18 per cent for females. Other studies, notably Rice (1986), also argue strongly for distinguishing between male and female school leavers.

A number of studies which have attempted to quantify the implications of reducing youth wages have found that the response of youth unemployment to changes in relative wages is small. For instance Lynch and Richardson (1982) reported that a one per cent fall in the relative costs of youth employment reduces the share of youth unemployment in total unemployment by only 1.3 per cent, so that in policy terms the importance of relative wages as a means of securing a reduction in total unemployment appears to be of limited importance. This is consistent with relative wages being a statistically significant factor in variations in relative youth unemployment because this does not necessarily imply a high elasticity of demand for labour.

At an international level the data are less refined and will not withstand the rigours of statistical analysis. However, a scatter diagram of the available data suggests that the West German case is an outlier compared with the European pattern. Figure 7.1 is derived from the data in Table 7.2 and relates to the average of initial and final apprentice remuneration as a percentage of the adult wage and the number of apprentices as a percentage of civil employment in the EEC in 1979.

FIGURE 7.1 AVERAGE OF INITIAL AND FINAL APPRENTICE REMUNERATION AS A PERCENTAGE OF ADULT WAGE AND APPRENTICES AS A PERCENTAGE OF CIVIL EMPLOYMENT IN THE EEC,1979.

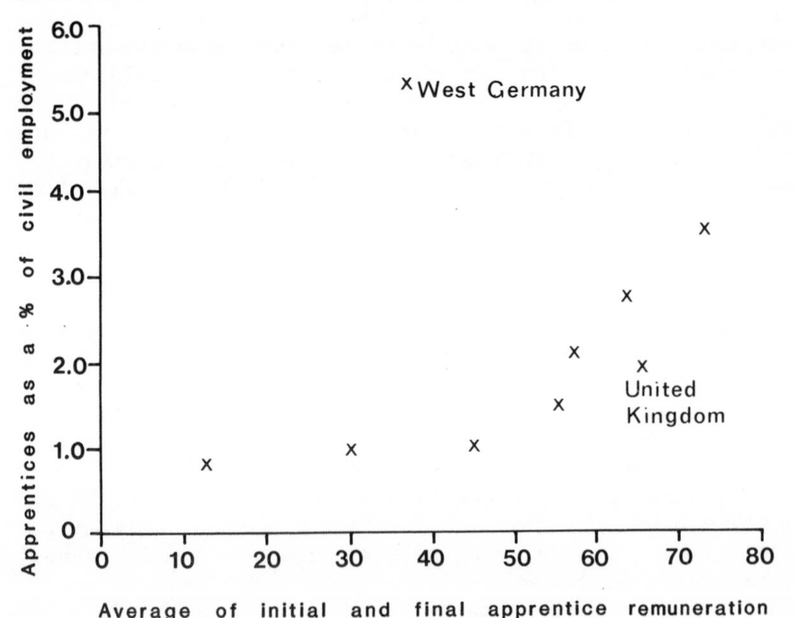

There is a positive association between the variables and this does not support the view that high remuneration discourages apprentice recruitment. On the other hand and by way of qualification, it must be borne in mind that the comparison of relative wages across international boundaries ignores both differing institutional arrangements and also variations in the degree of co-operation and unity between employers, unions and government.

The significance of this evidence is that it weakens the argument that lower relative wages are necessarily the main requirement for procuring more training by private firms. And even if a tenuous link has been established it may require an impracticable fall in relative wages to secure a significant increase in youth employment.

Arguably relative wages have been given more attention than they probably deserve in the development of training policies in the post-war period and this is particularly the case in the eighties. Many training schemes have become tarnished with the "cheap labour" image because training allowances are seen as a possible lever to encourage a reduction in the relative wage. School leavers, trade unions and employers have become wary and even antagonistic towards government schemes despite an initially high level of goodwill towards the intention of increasing the numbers in training, improving the quality of training opportunities and acquiring skills to augment the diversity and level of human capital.

8 Conclusions

The aspects of youth training that have been covered in previous chapters include the theory of training, specific recommendations for the development of the YTS and the measurement difficulties associated with its assessment.

Although some of the conclusions might also apply to past and future youth training measures, particularly those which include some elements of work experience and off-the-job training, it should be remembered that the evidence derived from the employers' surveys and the conclusions presented here are based on a period of severe demand restraint in the labour market and it may be inappropriate to extend these conclusions into alternative labour market regimes.

It has been argued that equilibrium in the labour market can be re-established either by greater wage flexibility or by shifts in the demand or supply of labour, and that the Government's current policy on youth training incorporates elements of both types of adjustment. However, there are two main problems with these solutions to the current difficulties in the youth labour market. First, it cannot be readily argued that wage flexibility is a proven remedy for youth unemployment and indirectly for the decline in youth training. While there may be some evidence to suggest that high relative youth wages may be <u>one</u> factor in rising relative youth unemployment, other evidence suggests that a substantial wage adjustment would be required to reduce significantly the youth unemployment rate. Second, it is inconsistent to pursue greater downward wage flexibility at the same time as an expansion in the skilled labour force when there is a general surfeit of labour if the objective is to re-establish the existing equilibrium wage. But if it is Government policy to lower the equilibrium wage itself, it is arguable that downward wage flexibility and an expansion in labour supply are mutually reinforcing. However, the main weakness in policy at the present time is on the demand side, and while there are obvious merits in formulating an integrated training strategy to prepare for a buoyant economic future, these must be balanced against the resource costs of wasting this investment through the failure to adopt effective demand management policies.

Finally recent policy emphasis on a market strategy towards the provision of training is an unproven method with a number of pitfalls which are rarely discussed and possibly ignored by the proponents of this approach. Two difficulties with the market strategy are the implications of relying on individuals to pursue the accumulation of human capital through the use of funds from imperfect capital markets and the distortions arising from the gap between the social rate of return on human capital and the private rate of return. For both these reasons the private sector may underprovide for the level of training particularly where there is a labour surplus.

YOUTH TRAINING RECOMMENDATIONS

These recommendations are limited to the main conclusions of Chapters Five, Six and Seven and some specific proposals which might alleviate the main drawbacks of the current YTS framework. There are four aspects of current youth training policy which seem to cause major difficulties for either employers ,trainees or the economy as a whole. First, the occupational structure of the YTS is heavily biased towards four OTF groups and particularly towards the clerical and personal services occupational families. This has implications for the economy in respect of manpower planning and also for the long term employment prospects of individual trainees who undertake training in these groups. Second, the method of financing training has been a constant dilemma for most of the period since the 1964 Act, and arguably the current policy of shifting on to employers an increasing proportion of the financial responsibility for training seems unlikely to succeed in the current state of the labour market. It is also evident that the provision of places in the former Mode B schemes cannot be subjected to the same accounting principles that were employed in the old Mode A schemes because of the need for excess provision in the former. Third, the levels of allowances for recent training schemes such as YOP and the YTS have created controversy; to some extent they have undermined the goodwill towards training and affected the public's assessment of the schemes. Fourth, although the extension of the YTS to two years has many advantages and has been generally welcomed by all sides of industry, it does appear to be the latest in a series of changes in training policy that have occurred in recent years. The usual rush towards early implementation might suggest to some that the novelty appeal of new schemes has superseded the real benefits of training policies.

It is arguable that a more positive approach than the one currently envisaged by the Government is necessary for alleviating some of these shortcomings and bridging the existing gap between the supply and demand for skills. Manpower planning is likely to be carried out more effectively through a system comparable to the ITB's whose detailed knowledge of the demand for skills in their own particular industries would be invaluable. It is suggested that YTS trainees who had been certificated at the end of their first year could be dove-tailed into ITB-organised courses to complete a further year of more industry-related training by 18 years of age. Cross-sector skills could be co-ordinated through a central agency like the MSC. There are three features in this proposal that are of critical importance. First, a second year that is industry-based rather than occupationally-based. This reflects the view that the demand for skills is derived from the demands for the goods and services those skills help to produce, and is essential for occupational forecasting. Second, there should be unconstrained movement of trainees between Occupational Training Families and the various industry-based programmes to help reduce any bias in the occupational structure of the YTS. Third, the training in both years should be entirely financed by government at least in the medium term and certainly in the prevailing economic climate.

MEASUREMENT PROBLEMS

The main measurement problems centre on the estimation of

the wastage rate and labour displacement, and in many respects the empirical analysis of both factors is less than ideal. However, data on wastage could be collected, at least in principle, on a more complete basis if this seemed worthwhile. The real difficulty is that it is unclear whether wastage rates have any policy significance for the success or failure of a scheme.

On the other hand the measurement of displacement is more involved and in need of further refinement if it is to be used in the development of policy measures. But evidence from the surveys does suggest that displacement is likely to be substantial, and this is not wholly unexpected given the current excess supply of labour in the economy. This reinforces the view that using scarce resources for training at a time of substantial labour surpluses may be a serious waste of resources in the absence of some policy to create more employment. If the latter is deemed to be beyond the scope of government policy then the economic case for investing in training is seriously weakened.

Bibliography

Becker, G.S. (1964). "Human Capital : A Theoretical and Empirical Analysis", National Bureau of Economic Research, New York.

Becker, G.S. (1975a). "Human Capital" , 2nd edition, Columbia University Press, New York.

Becker, G.S. (1975b). "The Allocation of Time Over the Life Cycle", in Ghez, G. and Becker, G. S. ,"The Allocation of Time and Goods Over the Life Cycle", pp.83-132, Columbia University Press, New York.

Blaug, M. (1968) (ed). "Economics of Education 1" ,Penguin Books, London, p.135.

Bolton, J.E. (1971). "Department of Trade and Industry Committee of Inquiry on Small Firms", Report, Cmnd 1811, HMSO, London.

Bushell, R. (1986). "The Evaluation of the Young Workers Scheme", Employment Gazette, Vol. 94, pp.145-152.

Cedefop (1981). "The Material and Social Standing of Young People During Transition from School to Working Life", Synthesis Report, Luxembourg.

Chapman, P.G. and Tooze, M.J. (1982). "The Displacement Effect : The Impact of Redundancies on Unemployment Duration", Applied Economics, Vol. 14, pp.31-41.

Chapman, P.G. and Tooze, M.J. (1985)."Youth Training in Scotland : A Review of Progress", Department of Economics, University of Dundee.

Chapman, P.G. and Tooze, M.J. (1986)."A Re-interview of Employers' Attitudes to the Youth Training Scheme in Dundee and Renfrew in 1985", Department of Economics, University of Dundee.

Committee on Scottish Affairs. (1981-1982). "Youth Unemployment and Training", HC96-1.

Department of Employment (1968). Employment Gazette, Vol. 76 ,p.334.

Department of Employment (1972). "Training for the Future : Plan for Discussion", London.

Department of Employment (1977a). Employment Gazette, Vol. 85 , pp.211-217.

Department of Employment (1977b). Employment Gazette, Vol. 85 , p.696.

Department of Employment (1978a). Employment Gazette, Vol. 86 , pp.294-297.

Department of Employment (1978b). Employment Gazette, Vol. 86 , pp.424-425.

Department of Employment (1980). Employment Gazette, Vol. 88, pp.946-947.

Department of Employment (1984). Employment Gazette, Vol. 92, p.477.

Department of Employment (1985). Employment Gazette, Vol. 93, pp.307-312.

Doeringer, P. B. and Piore, M. J. (1971). Internal Labour Markets and Manpower Analysis, prepared for the Manpower Administration, United States Department of Labour, Heath Press.

Dutton, P.A. (1982). "The New Training Initiative : What are its Chances?", Discussion Paper 18, University of Warwick, Institute of Employment Research, Coventry.

Gershuny, J. and Miles, I. (1983) "The New Service Economy: The Transformation of Employment in Industrial Societies", Pinter, London.

Greaves, K., Gostyn, P. and Bonsall, C. (1982). "Off-the-Job Training on YOP : A Summary of Research Findings in Work Experience Schemes 1972-1982", Research and Development Series No. 12, MSC, London.

Hayes, C., et. al (1984). "Training for Skill Ownership :Learning to Take it with You", Institute of Manpower Studies,Universtiy of Sussex.

HMSO (1984). "Youth Training in the EEC", Select Committee on the European Communities, House of Lords, 24th Report, Session 1983-84.

Hughes, J. J. (1972). "The Roles of Manpower Retraining Programmes: A critical look at retraining in the United Kingdom", British Journal of Industrial Relations, Vol.X, pp.206-223.

Hutchinson, Gillian, Barr, N. A. and Drobny, A. (1984). " A Sequential Approach to the Dynamic Specification of the Demand for Young Male Labour in Great Britain", Applied Economics, Vol. 16,pp.187-204.

Johnson, P.S. (1971). "The Economics of Training and the Industrial Training Boards", Moorgate and Wall Street, Autumn, p.63.

Jones, I. (1982). "The New Training Initiative - An Education", National Institute Economic Review, No. 99, February, pp.68-74.

Killingsworth, M.R. (1983). "Labour Supply", Cambridge University Press.

Layard, R. (1979), "The Costs and Benefits of Selective Employment Policies : The British Case", British Journal of Industrial Relations, Vol. XVII, pp.187-204.

Layard, R. (1982). "Youth Unemployment in Britain and the US Compared", in Freeman, R. and Wise D. (eds) "The Youth Labour Market Problem", NBER, University of Chicago,pp.499-542.

Layard, R. and Nickell, S. (1980). "The Case for Subsidising Extra Jobs", Economic Journal, Vol. 98, pp.51-73.

Lees, D. and Chiplin, B. (1970). "The Economics of Industrial Training", Lloyds Bank Review, April, pp.29-41.

Lindley, R.M. (1980). "Employment Policy in Transition", in Lindley, R.M. "Economic Change and Employment Policy", Macmillan , London and Basingstoke, pp.330-382.

Lindley, R.M. (1983). "Active Manpower Policy",in Bain, G.S., "Industrial Relations in Britain", Oxford : Blackwell, pp.339-360.

Lynch, Lisa M. (1984). "State Dependency in Youth Unemployment : A Lost Generation?", Centre for Labour Economics ,London School of Economics, Working Paper No. 184 (January).

Lynch, Lisa M. and Richardson, Ray (1982). "Unemployment of Young Workers in Great Britain", British Journal of Industrial Relations ,Vol. 20, No. 1, pp.362-372.

Magnussen, O. (1979). "The Opportunity Structure for Early School Leavers in Member States", Part 3 in Cedefop (1979), "Youth unemployment and Vocational Training : Occupational Choice , Motivation of Young People , Their Vocational Training and Employment Prospects", Luxembourg.

Main, B.G.M. (1985). "Earnings,Expected Earnings,and Unemployment Among School Leavers", University of Edinburgh Discussion Paper Series.

Makeham, P. (1980). "Youth Unemployment : An Examination of the Evidence on Youth Unemployment Using National Statistics", Research Paper No. 10, London : Department of Employment.

Ministry of Labour (1962). "Industrial Training: Government Proposals", Cmnd,1892, London.

MSC (1977). "Young People And Work" ,The Holland Report, London.

MSC (1980). "Outlook on Training : Review of the Employment and Training Act 1973", London.

MSC (1981a). "A New Training Initiative : A Consultative Document, London.

MSC (1981b). "A New Training Initiative : An Agenda for Action", London.

MSC (1982a). "A New Training Initiative : A Programme for Action",Cmnd. 8455, p.50.

MSC (1982b). "Youth Task Group Report", London.

Oatey, M. (1970). "The Economics of Training with Respect to the Firm", British Journal of Industrial Relations, Vol. VIII, pp.1-21.

Raffe, D. (1984). in D. McCrone (ed) "Scottish Government Yearbook, 1984", Unit for the Study of Government in Scotland, University of Edinburgh.

Rice, P.G. (1986). "Juvenile Unemployment, Relative Unemployment and Social Security in Great Britain", Economic Journal, Vol. 96, pp.352-374.

Roberts, K. (1984). "School Leavers and their Prospects : Youth in the 1980's", Open University Press, Milton Keynes.

Roberts, K.,Dench, S. and Richardson, D. (1986). "Youth Labour Markets in the 1980's", Employment Gazette, Vol. 94, pp.241-246.

Robinson, O. (1985). "The Changing Labour Market : The Phenomenon of Part-Time Employment in Britain", National Westminster Bank Quarterly Review, London.

Robinson, O. and Wallace, J. (1984). "Growth and Utililsation of Part-Time Labour in Great Britain", Employment Gazette, Vol. 92, pp.391-397.

Sako, Mari and Dore, Ronald (1986). "How the Youth Training Scheme Helps Employers", Employment Gazette, Vol. 92, pp.195-204.

Thurow, L. (1970). "Investment in Human Capital", Wadsworth ,Belmont, California.

Times Educational Supplement, Times Newspapers Ltd., London, January 6, 1984.

Wells, William (1983). "The Relative Pay and Employment of Young People", Department of Employment, Research Paper No. 42 , December.

Williams, V. (1984). "Employment Implications of New Technology", Employment Gazette, Vol. 92, pp.210-215.

Youthaid (1981). "Quality or Collapse?", London.

Youth Training News , No. 10, April 1984.

Tables and chart

TABLE 1.1 : NUMBERS AND PERCENTAGES OF RESPONDENTS IN THE DUNDEE-RENFREW SURVEY FOR 1984 (WITH 1984 TRAINEES) WHO ALSO PARTICIPATED IN THE 1985 ENQUIRY, BY SIZE OF ESTABLISHMENT.

SIZE OF ESTABLISHMENT	TRAINEES		RESPONDENTS	
	N	%	N	%
0-10 Employees	34	11.9	31	35.2
11-25 "	40	14.0	19	21.6
26-50 "	17	6.0	9	10.2
51-100 "	37	13.0	7	8.0
101-250 "	65	22.8	15	17.0
251-500 "	6	2.1	1	1.1
501-1000 "	11	3.9	2	2.3
Over 1000 "	75	26.3	4	4.5
TOTAL	285	100.0	88	100.0

Source: Chapman P.G. and Tooze M.J., 1986.

TABLE 1.2 : NUMBERS AND PERCENTAGES OF RESPONDENTS IN THE DUNDEE-RENFREW SURVEY FOR 1984 (WITH 1984 TRAINEES) WHO ALSO PARTICIPATED IN THE 1985 ENQUIRY, BY OCCUPATIONAL TRAINING FAMILY.

OCCUPATIONAL TRAINING FAMILY	TRAINEES		RESPONDENTS	
	N	%	N	%
1 Clerical	74	27.2	22	25.3
2 Agriculture/ Horticulture	2	0.7	1	1.1
3 Craft and Design	3	1.1	3	3.4
4 Installation, Maintenance and Repair	56	20.6	16	18.4
5 Technical and Scientific	10	3.7	3	3.4
6 Manufacturing and Assembly	36	13.2	10	11.5
7 Processing	5	1.8	2	2.3
8 Food Processing	-	-	-	-
9 Personal Services and Sales	74	27.2	26	29.9
10 Community & Health	-	-	-	-
11 Transport	12	4.4	4	4.6
TOTAL	272	100.0	87	100.0

Source: Chapman P.G. and Tooze M.J., 1986.

TABLE 1.3 : NUMBERS AND PERCENTAGES OF RESPONDENTS IN THE DUNDEE-RENFREW SURVEY FOR 1984 (WITH 1984 TRAINEES) WHO ALSO PARTICIPATED IN THE 1985 ENQUIRY, BY ORGANISATIONAL STRUCTURE OF COMPANY.

TYPE OF ORGANISATION	TRAINEES		RESPONDENTS	
	N	%	N	%
Sole Place of Trade	85	29.8	35	39.8
Part of Local Group	85	29.8	14	15.9
Part of National Group	90	31.6	28	31.8
Part of an International Group (British Owned)	8	2.8	6	6.8
Part of an International Group (Foreign Owned)	17	6.0	5	5.7
TOTAL	285	100.0	88	100.0

Source: Chapman P.G. and Tooze M.J., 1986.

TABLE 1.4 : REASONS FOR REDUCING THE NUMBER OF YTS TRAINEES IN 1984-85.

REASON FOR REDUCING NUMBERS OF TRAINEES	NUMBER OF RESPONDENTS
Not Interested	8
Company too Small	9
Temporary Reduction	8
Unfilled Vacancies	8
Trade Union Opposition	3
Redundancies	2
TOTAL	38

Source: Chapman P.G. and Tooze M.J., 1986.

TABLE 3.1 : NUMBERS OF APPRENTICES AND OTHER TRAINEES IN GREAT BRITAIN, 1981-86 (THOUSAND) FOR MANUFACTURING INDUSTRIES.

Date	Apprentices			Other Trainees		
	Male	Female	Total	Male	Female	Total
March 1981	143.2	4.4	147.6	41.7	21.2	62.9
March 1982	119.8	3.9	123.7	34.7	21.3	56.0
March 1983	99.0	3.4	102.4	30.1	17.8	47.9
March 1984	77.3	4.7	82.0	23.4	16.2	39.7
March 1985	69.1	4.1	73.2	23.4	15.7	39.2
March 1986	59.7	4.0	63.7	24.1	14.2	38.2

Source : Employment Gazette.

TABLE 3.2 : APPRENTICES AND OTHER TRAINEES AS A PROPORTION OF EMPLOYEES FOR GREAT BRITAIN, 1981-86 FOR MANUFACTURING INDUSTRIES.

Date	Apprentices (%)			Other Trainees (%)		
	Male	Female	Total	Male	Female	Total
March 1981	3.3	0.3	2.4	1.0	1.2	1.0
March 1982	2.9	0.2	2.2	0.9	1.3	1.0
March 1983	2.6	0.2	1.9	0.8	1.2	0.9
March 1984	2.0	0.3	1.5	0.6	1.0	0.7
March 1985	1.8	0.3	1.4	0.6	1.0	0.7
March 1986	1.6	0.3	1.2	0.6	0.1	0.7

Source : Employment Gazette.

TABLE 3.3 : APPRENTICES AND TRAINEES IN MANUFACTURING INDUSTRIES FOR GREAT BRITAIN FOR 1970-85(THOUSAND) AND AS A PERCENTAGE OF EMPLOYEES.

	Apprentices	Other Trainees	Total
MALE			
1970	211.6 (3.8%)	121.9 (2.2%)	333.5 (5.0%)
1975	151.4 (2.9%)	84.4 (1.6%)	235.8 (4.5%)
1980	144.8 (3.1%)	57.4 (1.2%)	202.2 (4.4%)
1985	69.1 (1.8%)	23.4 (0.6%)	92.6 (2.4%)
FEMALE			
1970	7.0 (0.3%)	80.2 (3.2%)	87.2 (3.5%)
1975	3.9 (0.2%)	50.8 (2.3%)	54.7 (2.5%)
1980	4.7 (0.2%)	32.6 (1.7%)	37.3 (1.9%)
1985	4.1 (0.3%)	15.7 (1.0%)	19.8 (1.3%)

Source : Employment Gazette.

TABLE 3.4 : APPRENTICES BY INDUSTRIAL ORDER FOR GREAT BRITAIN FOR 1970-85 (THOUSAND) AND AS A PERCENTAGE OF EMPLOYEES(a).

<table>
<tr><th>ORDER</th><th>DESCRIPTION</th><th>1970</th><th>1975</th><th>1980</th><th>1985(b)</th></tr>
<tr><td>III</td><td>Food, Drink & Tobacco</td><td>4.0
(0.5%)</td><td>3.7
(0.5%)</td><td>3.1
(0.5%)</td><td>2.1
(0.4%)</td></tr>
<tr><td>IV</td><td>Petroleum</td><td>1.2
(2.4%)</td><td>0.8
(2.1%)</td><td>0.8
(2.2%)</td><td>n.a</td></tr>
<tr><td>V</td><td>Chemicals & Allied Industries</td><td>5.1
(1.2%)</td><td>3.7
(0.9%)</td><td>5.5
(1.3%)</td><td>2.3
(0.7%)</td></tr>
<tr><td>VI</td><td>Metal Manufacture</td><td>13.2
(2.4%)</td><td>12.5
(2.5%)</td><td>11.1
(2.7%)</td><td>n.a</td></tr>
<tr><td>VII</td><td>Mechanical Engineering</td><td>62.6
(5.5%)</td><td>38.2
(4.0%)</td><td>39.5
(4.6%)</td><td>15.9
(2.1%)</td></tr>
<tr><td>VIII</td><td>Instrument Engineering</td><td>4.2
(2.9%)</td><td>2.3
(1.5%)</td><td>3.4
(2.4%)</td><td>1.6
(1.6%)</td></tr>
<tr><td>IX</td><td>Electrical Engineering</td><td>24.1
(2.8%)</td><td>13.7
(1.8%)</td><td>18.4
(2.0%)</td><td>11.9
(1.7%)</td></tr>
<tr><td>X</td><td>Shipbuilding & Marine Engineering</td><td>11.6
(7.9%)</td><td>9.8
(6.8%)</td><td>1.7
(7.1%)</td><td>n.a</td></tr>
<tr><td>XI</td><td>Vehicles</td><td>31.7
(3.9%)</td><td>22.8
(3.0%)</td><td>27.0
(3.8%)</td><td>5.9
(2.1%)</td></tr>
<tr><td>XII</td><td>Metal Goods not elsewhere specified</td><td>17.1
(2.9%)</td><td>11.3
(2.1%)</td><td>11.4
(2.3%)</td><td>4.0
(1.1%)</td></tr>
<tr><td>XIII</td><td>Textiles</td><td>5.0
(0.8%)</td><td>2.9
(0.6%)</td><td>2.4
(0.6%)</td><td>n.a</td></tr>
<tr><td>XIV</td><td>Leather, Leather Goods & Fur</td><td>0.3
(0.6%)</td><td>0.3
(0.8%)</td><td>0.2
(0.7%)</td><td rowspan="2">0.8
(0.2%)</td></tr>
<tr><td>XV</td><td>Clothing & Footwear</td><td>3.6
(0.8%)</td><td>2.0
(0.5%)</td><td>1.3
(0.4%)</td></tr>
</table>

TABLE 3.4 (Contd) : APPRENTICES BY INDUSTRIAL ORDER FOR GREAT BRITAIN FOR 1970-85(THOUSAND) AND AS A PERCENTAGE OF EMPLOYEES(a).

ORDER	DESCRIPTION	1970	1975	1980	1985(b)
XVI	Bricks, Pottery, Glass & Cement	4.0 (1.3%)	3.1 (1.1%)	3.0 (1.2%)	n.a
XVII	Timber & Furniture	4.5 (3.8%)	11.3 (4.3%)	8.1 (3.3%)	4.2 (2.0%)
XVIII	Paper, Printing & Publishing	18.6 (3.2%)	14.5 (2.6%)	9.8 (1.9%)	3.7 (0.8%)
XIX	Other Manufacturing Industries	2.9 (0.9%)	2.4 (0.7%)	2.9 (1.0%)	3.4 (0.5%)
ALL MANUFACTURING INDUSTRIES		218.6 (2.7%)	155.3 (2.1%)	149.5 (2.3%)	73.2 (1.4%)

Notes : (a) - These figures are also available by sex.

(b) - The 1985 figures are not directly comparable, but figures are given where available.

Source : Employment Gazette.

TABLE 3.5 : OTHER TRAINEES BY INDUSTRIAL ORDER FOR GREAT BRITAIN FOR 1970-85 (THOUSAND) AND AS A PERCENTAGE OF EMPLOYEES(a).

ORDER	DESCRIPTION	1970	1975	1980	1985(b)
III	Food, Drink & Tobacco	18.0 (2.4%)	8.7 (1.2%)	4.4 (0.7%)	1.4 (0.2%)
IV	Petroleum	0.8 (1.5%)	0.4 (1.1%)	0.4 (1.0%)	n.a
V	Chemicals & Allied Industries	12.9 (2.9%)	7.1 (1.7%)	4.8 (1.1%)	2.0 (0.6%)
VI	Metal Manufacture	12.8 (2.3%)	6.0 (1.2%)	5.6 (1.4%)	n.a
VII	Mechanical Engineering	27.1 (2.4%)	18.2 (1.9%)	12.6 (1.5%)	5.4 (0.7%)
VIII	Instrument Engineering	4.0 (2.7%)	3.5 (2.3%)	2.6 (1.8%)	1.2 (1.2%)
IX	Electrical Engineering	23.9 (2.8%)	18.6 (2.4%)	10.6 (1.5%)	7.2 (1.1%)
X	Shipbuilding & Marine Engineering	1.1 (0.7%)	0.7 (0.5%)	0.1 (0.3%)	n.a
XI	Vehicles	11.7 (1.4%)	8.5 (1.1%)	5.8 (0.8%)	1.8 (0.6%)
XII	Metal Goods not elsewhere specified	19.6 (3.3%)	15.4 (2.8%)	8.9 (1.8%)	2.7 (0.7%)
XIII	Textiles	14.2 (2.2%)	8.8 (1.7%)	5.4 (1.3%)	n.a
XIV	Leather, Leather Goods & Fur	1.8 (3.6%)	0.9 (2.1%)	0.6 (1.9%)	4.7 (1.5%)
XV	Clothing & Footwear	17.3 (3.9%)	12.2 (3.1%)	9.4 (2.8%)	

TABLE 3.5 : OTHER TRAINEES BY INDUSTRIAL ORDER FOR GREAT
(Contd) BRITAIN FOR 1970-85 (THOUSAND) AND AS A PERCENTAGE OF EMPLOYEES(a).

ORDER	DESCRIPTION	1970	1975	1980	1985(b)
XVI	Bricks, Pottery, Glass & Cement	7.3 (2.4%)	7.1 (2.5%)	3.3 (1.4%)	n.a
XVII	Timber & Furniture	6.3 (2.5%)	5.7 (2.2%)	4.1 (1.7%)	2.0 (1.0%)
XVIII	Paper, Printing & Publishing	15.3 (2.0%)	9.0 (1.7%)	8.3 (1.6%)	3.1 (0.7%)
XIX	Other Manufacturing Industries	8.3 (2.6%)	3.6 (1.1%)	3.1 (1.1%)	5.0 (0.7%)
ALL MANUFACTURING INDUSTRIES		202.1 (2.5%)	135.2 (1.8%)	90.0 (1.4%)	39.2 (0.7%)

Notes : (a) - These figures are also available by sex.

(b) - The 1985 figures are not directly comparable ,but figures are given where available.

Source : Employment Gazette.

TABLE 3.6 : APPRENTICES (MANUAL AND NON-MANUAL) AS A PERCENTAGE OF ALL EMPLOYEES FOR EEC MEMBER COUNTRIES IN 1978 AND 1981 (ALL INDUSTRIES).

	1978 %	1981 %
West Germany	4.8	5.9
France	0.3	0.4
Italy	1.0	1.0
Netherlands	0.8	0.9
Belgium	0.6	0.7
Luxembourg	1.8	1.7
United Kingdom	3.5	3.7
Ireland	4.4	4.4
Denmark	3.9	3.8
Greece	-	0.2

Source : Labour Costs, Eurostat.

TABLE 3.7 : APPRENTICES (MANUAL AND NON-MANUAL) AS A PERCENTAGE OF ALL EMPLOYEES FOR EEC MEMBER COUNTRIES IN 1978 AND 1981 (MANUFACTURING INDUSTRIES).

	1978 %	1981 %
West Germany	4.3	5.1
France	0.2	0.2
Italy	1.1	1.0
Netherlands	0.6	0.7
Belgium	0.6	0.7
Luxembourg	1.7	1.4
United Kingdom	3.2	3.1
Ireland	4.4	4.3
Denmark	2.9	2.9
Greece	-	0.2

Source : Labour Costs, Eurostat.

TABLE 3.8 : UNEMPLOYMENT RATES BY AGE FOR THE UNITED KINGDOM AND TOTAL FOR GREAT BRITAIN, MALE AND FEMALE, 1983-86.

	UNITED KINGDOM			GREAT BRITAIN
Year	Under 18		All ages	All Ages
	April	Annual Average	April	April
	%	%	%	%
1983	24.6	24.4	13.2	13.1
1984	16.8	19.5	12.8	12.7
1985	16.8	19.0	13.5	13.3
1986	19.0	19.0*	13.7	13.6

Notes : * - Average figure for January and April.

Source : Employment Gazette.

TABLE 3.9 : UNITED KINGDOM UNEMPLOYMENT DURATION BY AGE (THOUSAND) AND PROPORTION IN TOTAL UNEMPLOYMENT IN GREAT BRITAIN FOR MALES AND FEMALES, APRIL 1983-86.

Age Group	1983	1984	1985	1986
	Unemployment Duration : Up to 26 weeks			
17 and under	143.3 (4.7%)	92.9 (3.1%)	93.7 (2.9%)	123.5 (3.9%)
18	91.4 (3.0%)	77.1 (2.6%)	76.6 (2.4%)	71.3 (2.2%)
19	70.2 (2.3%)	72.8 (2.4%)	72.9 (2.3%)	70.3 (2.2%)
20-24	263.5 (8.6%)	269.1 (9.0%)	287.0 (9.0%)	287.3 (9.0%)
25 and over	698.1 (22.9%)	663.2 (22.2%)	681.4 (21.4%)	709.2 (22.2%)
All ages	1266.5 (41.3%)	1175.1 (39.3%)	1211.6 (38.0%)	1261.6 (39.4%)

TABLE 3.9 (Contd) : UNITED KINGDOM UNEMPLOYMENT DURATION BY AGE (THOUSAND) AND PROPORTION IN TOTAL UNEMPLOYMENT IN GREAT BRITAIN FOR MALES AND FEMALES, APRIL 1983-86.

Age Group	1983	1984	1985	1986
Unemployment Duration : Over 26 and up to 52 weeks				
17 and under	47.9 (1.6%)	48.0 (1.6%)	51.2 (1.6%)	46.5 (1.5%)
18	55.5 (1.8%)	56.1 (1.9%)	50.8 (1.6%)	43.5 (1.4%)
19	70.2 (1.6%)	72.8 (1.6%)	72.9 (1.1%)	70.1 (1.2%)
20-24	144.3 (4.7%)	137.3 (4.6%)	149.7 (4.7%)	140.1 (4.4%)
25 and over	398.1 (13.0%)	362.9 (12.1%)	380.7 (11.9%)	372.6 (11.6%)
All ages	693.8 (22.7%)	651.4 (21.8%)	666.4 (20.9%)	641.7 (20.1%)

TABLE 3.9 (Contd) : UNITED KINGDOM UNEMPLOYMENT DURATION BY AGE (THOUSAND) AND PROPORTION IN TOTAL UNEMPLOYMENT IN GREAT BRITAIN FOR MALES AND FEMALES, APRIL 1983-86.

Age Group	1983	1984	1985	1986
	Unemployment Duration : Over 52 weeks			
17 and under	9.7 (0.3%)	14.7 (0.5%)	11.4 (0.4%)	11.5 (0.4%)
18	34.4 (1.1%)	42.0 (1.9%)	38.4 (1.7%)	32.4 (1.4%)
19	50.6 (1.7%)	56.2 (1.9%)	55.6 (1.7%)	45.5 (1.4%)
20-24	191.2 (6.3%)	219.2 (7.3%)	235.5 (7.4%)	246.9 (7.7%)
25 and over	807.3 (26.4%)	829.0 (27.7%)	967.7 (30.4%)	959.3 (30.0%)
All ages	1093.2 (35.8%)	1161.1 (38.9%)	1308.6 (41.1%)	1295.6 (40.5%)
TOTAL FOR GREAT BRITAIN	3053.5	2987.6	3186.2	3198.9

Source: Employment Gazette.

TABLE 5.1 : UNIFIED VOCATIONAL PREPARATION IN SCOTLAND, 1977-83.

YEAR	NO. OF SCHEMES COMMENCING	NO. OF INDUSTRIES PARTICIPATING	NO. OF YOUNG PEOPLE COMPLETING COURSES
1977	2	2	22
1978	5	2	49
1979	27	7	365
1980	39	15	472
1981(a)	21	9	266(b)
1981-82(c)	78	14	1041
1982-83(c)	43	21	528

Notes : (a) - The 1981 figure relates to the period from 1 January to 31 March.

(b) - Total relates to young people starting courses.

(c) - April to March inclusive.

Source : Manpower Services Commission.

TABLE 5.2 : AVERAGE QUARTERLY NUMBERS SUPPORTED BY SPECIAL EMPLOYMENT AND TRAINING MEASURES IN GREAT BRITAIN, 1975-86 (THOUSAND).

	1975-76 (a)	1976-77	1977-78	1978-79	1979-80	1980-81
RSSL	7.5	5.0	-	-	-	-
YES	-	3.0	8.5	3.3	-	-
CI	1.8	3.2	4.2	3.8	5.8	6.2
TI	7.7	26.2	28.7	27.2	19.3	14.0
JCP	1.4	21.0	36.7	17.7	-	-
WEP	-	1.8	19.6	-	-	-
YOP	-	-	-	35.3	77.3	141.3
YTS	-	-	-	-	-	-
YWS	-	-	-	-	-	-
NWS	-	-	-	-	-	-

KEY :

RSSL - Recruitment Subsidy for School-Leavers
YES - Youth Employment Subsidy
CI - Community Industry
TI - Training Places supported in Industry
JCP - Job Creation Programme
WEP - Work Experience Programme
YOP - Youth Opportunities Programme
YTS - Youth Training Scheme
YWS - Young Workers Scheme
NWS - New Workers Scheme

1981-82	1982-83	1983-84	1984-85	1985-86	1986-87 (b)
-	-	-	-	-	-
-	-	-	-	-	-
6.7	7.0	7.0	6.9	5.1	8.0
19.6	17.3	8.8	1.7	1.1	-
-	-	-	-	-	-
-	-	-	-	-	-
199.7	240.0	35.6	-	-	-
-	-	156.3	283.5	214.7	280.2 (c)
8.2	100.1	103.9	69.5	38.7	35.3
-	-	-	-	-	n.a.

Notes: (a) - April to March inclusive.

(b) - April to June 1986 inclusive.

(c) - Total number of young people in training on June 30, 1986.

Sources: Manpower Services Commission
Employment Gazette.

TABLE 5.3 : YOUTH OPPORTUNITIES PROGRAMME IN GREAT BRITAIN : ENTRANTS BY SCHEME TYPE IN 1978-83(THOUSAND).

	NUMBER OF ENTRANTS	
	1978-79 (a)	1979-80
Work experience on employers' premises	108.4	138.9
Project based work experience	8.4	15.2
Community Service	7.6	20.7
Training Workshops	3.8	7.3
TOTAL WORK EXPERIENCE	128.2	168.1
Employment induction courses	2.4	3.0
Short training courses	30.9	29.3
Remedial and Preparatory courses	0.7	2.0
TOTAL WORK PREPARATION	34.0	34.3

Notes : (a) - April-March inclusive.

(b) - Community Service and Project based work experience merged to become Community Projects in April 1981.

Source : MSC Annual Reports.

NUMBER OF ENTRANTS		
1980-81	1981-82	1982-83
242.0	371.2	309.4
20.1	74.1 (b)	68.3(b)
30.2		
12.0	16.2	15.7
304.3	461.5	393.4
4.1	3.7	3.2
51.4	87.8	64.6
55.5	91.5	67.8

TABLE 6.1 : APPROVED PLACES AND STARTS ON THE YTS BY OCCUPATIONAL TRAINING FAMILY FOR GREAT BRITAIN, 1984-85.

OTF	DESCRIPTION	APPROVED PLACES	STARTS MODE A
		%	%
1	Administrative, Clerical and Office	19	22
2	Agriculture, Horticulture, Forestry and Fisheries	5	4
3	Craft and Design	5	3
4	Installation, Maintenance and Repair	14	13
5	Technical and Scientific	3	2
6	Manufacturing and Assembly	17	15
7	Processing	1	1
8	Food Processing	5	4
9	Personal Services and Sales	18	23
10	Community and Health Services	4	2
11	Transport Services	2	2
	Unclassified *	7	9
		100	100
	TOTAL (THOUSAND)	396.0	228.5

Note : * - Some schemes offered a general range of training and cannot be classified to a single family. Also many trainees, particularly on Mode B schemes, started in a broad based assessment, and no single OTF was recorded.

STARTS				
MODE B1			MODE B2	
Community Projects %	Training Workshops %	Information & Technology Centres %	%	ALL STARTS %
5	6	32	7	18
6	9	-	2	4
9	9	-	2	4
17	8	6	15	13
-	1	29	2	2
8	28	5	12	14
-	-	-	1	1
2	4	-	5	4
1	-	-	5	17
14	-	-	6	4
-	-	-	1	2
36	40	29	41	17
100	100	100	100	100
57.8	25.9	6.7	16.2	395.1

Sources: Youth Training News
Employment Gazette.

TABLE 6.2 : PROPORTION OF TOTAL ENTRANTS TO THE YTS IN MODE A SCHEMES AND UNEMPLOYMENT RATE BY REGION, APRIL 1984-MARCH 1985.

REGION	% IN MODE A	REGIONAL UNEMPLOYMENT RATE (a)
Scotland	75.3	15.2
Northern	60.2	18.5
North West	67.8	16.0
Yorkshire & Humberside	69.9	14.5
Midlands	75.8	14.3
Wales	66.8	16.5
South West	79.9	11.6
London and South East (b)	78.9	9.7

Notes : (a) - Average Monthly Rates

(b) - Including East Anglia

Source: Employment Gazette.

TABLE 6.3 : OCCUPATIONAL TRAINING FAMILIES AND THEIR KEY PURPOSES.

OTF NO.	OCCUPATIONS	KEY PURPOSE
1	Administrative, Clerical and Office Services	Information processing
2	Agriculture, Horticulture, Forestry and Fisheries	Nurturing and gathering living resources
3	Craft and Design	Creating single or small numbers of objects using hand or power tools
4	Installation, Maintenance and Repair	Applying known procedures for making equipment work
5	Technical and Scientific	Applying known principles to making things work or usable
6	Manufacturing and Assembly	Transforming metallic and non-metallic materials through shaping, construction and assembly into products
7	Processing	Intervening in the working of machines when necessary
8	Food Preparation and Service	Handling and transforming edible matter
9	Personal Services and Sales	Satisfying the needs of individual customers

TABLE 6.3 : OCCUPATIONAL TRAINING FAMILIES AND THEIR KEY PURPOSES.
(Contd)

OTF NO.	OCCUPATIONS	KEY PURPOSE
10	Community and Health Services	Meeting socially defined needs of the community
11	Transport services	Moving goods or people

Source: Hayes, C. et al (1983).

TABLE 6.4 : NUMBERS OF ENTRANTS AND PLACES FOR ALL YTS SCHEMES IN GREAT BRITAIN, 1983-86.

	PLANNED ENTRANTS	APPROVED PLACES	ENTRANTS TO TRAINING	IN TRAINING AT END OF PERIOD
1983-84	459,770	442,495	353,979	-
1984-85	404,560	-	389,360	271,059
1985-86	384,295	-	398,704	265,219

Source: Employment Gazette.

CHART 6.1: DESIGN FRAMEWORK FOR THE TWO-YEAR YTS

Training content to be delivered through integrated

INPUTS

Planned work experience and on-the-job training	Off-the-job training/education

expressed in a

Training Plan with Competence Objectives

delivered through

TRAINING PROCESSES

Induction and initial assessment
Participation and learning
Continuous assessment
Guidance/reviewing

to produce

THESE OUTCOMES

Competence in a job and/or a range of occupational skills	Competence in a range of transferable core skills	Ability to transfer skills and knowledge to new situations	Personal effectiveness

which lead to

CERTIFICATION

Vocational qualifications,demonstrating occupational competence,or credit towards such qualifications;plus a record of achievement

Source : Youth Training News.

TABLE 7.1 : PERCENTAGE OF TRAINEES REMAINING ON THE YTS IN DUNDEE AND RENFREW IN 1984-85, BY TOTAL, SEX AND VOLUNTARY/INVOLUNTARY.

% REMAINING AFTER	TOTAL	MALE	FEMALE	VOLUNTARY	INVOLUNTARY
	100.0%	100.0%	100.0%	100.0%	100.0%
2 Weeks	97.0	95.8	97.5	98.5	98.5
4 "	93.9	95.8	90.8	95.8	98.1
6 "	91.6	95.0	86.6	94.7	97.0
8 "	90.1	93.3	84.9	93.5	96.6
10 "	90.1	93.3	84.9	93.5	96.6
12 "	90.1	93.3	84.9	93.5	96.6
14 "	89.0	91.7	84.0	93.2	95.8
16 "	88.6	90.8	84.0	93.2	95.4
18 "	88.6	90.8	84.0	93.2	95.4
20 "	88.2	90.0	84.0	92.8	95.4
22 "	87.8	89.2	84.0	92.8	95.1
24 "	87.8	89.2	84.0	92.8	95.1
26 "	86.7	87.5	83.2	91.6	95.1
28 "	86.7	87.5	83.2	91.6	95.1
30 "	86.7	87.5	83.2	91.6	95.1
32 "	86.7	87.5	83.2	91.6	95.1
34 "	86.7	87.5	83.2	91.6	95.1
36 "	86.7	86.7	83.2	91.2	95.1
38 "	85.9	85.8	83.2	91.2	94.7
40 "	85.2	84.2	83.2	90.5	94.7
42 "	85.2	84.2	83.2	90.5	94.7
44 "	84.8	83.3	83.2	90.5	94.3
46 "	84.4	82.5	83.2	90.1	94.3

Source: Chapman P.G. and Tooze M.J., 1986.

TABLE 7.2 : INITIAL AND FINAL APPRENTICE REMUNERATION EXPRESSED AS A PERCENTAGE OF THE ADULT WAGE AND THE NUMBER OF APPRENTICES EXPRESSED AS A PERCENTAGE OF CIVIL EMPLOYMENT IN THE EEC, 1979-80.

COUNTRY	INITIAL (1) AND FINAL (2) REMUNERATION AS A PERCENTAGE OF ADULT WAGE *		APPRENTICES AS A PERCENTAGE OF CIVIL EMPLOYMENT
	(1)	(2)	
Belgium	5	20	0.8
Denmark	25	90	2.2
West Germany	30	45	5.2
France	15	45	1.0
Ireland	30	80	1.6
Italy	55	90	3.6
Luxembourg	50	75	2.7
Netherlands	28	62	1.1
United Kingdom	40	90	1.9

Notes: * - It should be noted that a number of figures for apprentice remuneration are based on minimum statutory rates and specific industry rates.

Source: Cedefop (1981).

Author index

Subject index